WILD NATURE
WON BY KINDNESS

BY

MRS. BRIGHTWEN, F.Z.S., F.E.S.

Vice-President of the Selborne Society.

NEW WEST PRESS

Copyright © 2021 by New West Press

ISBN 978-1-64965-156-3

All rights reserved. This book or any portion thereof may not be reproduced or used in any manner whatsoever without the express written permission of the publisher except for the use of brief quotations in a book review or scholarly journal.

New West Press
Henderson, NV 89052
www.nwwst com

Ordering Information:
Special discounts are available on quantity purchases by corporations, associations, educators, and others. For details, contact the publisher at the listed address below.

U.S. trade bookstores and wholesalers: Please contact New West Press:

Tel: (480) 648-1061; or email: contact@nwwst.com

To

SIR JAMES PAGET, BART., F.R.S., D.C.L., Etc., Etc.

MY DEAR SIR JAMES,—

The little papers which are here reprinted would scarcely have been written but for the encouragement of your sympathy and the stimulus of what you have contributed to the loving study of nature. Shall you, then, think me presumptuous if I venture to dedicate to the friend what I could never dream of presenting to the professor, and if I ask you to pardon the poorness of the gift in consideration of the sincerity with which it is given.

    Pray believe me to be
      Yours very sincerely,
        ELIZA BRIGHTWEN.

THE GROVE, GREAT STANMORE.
 June, 1800.

TABLE OF CONTENTS

INTRODUCTION...1

1. REARING BIRDS FROM THE NEST. 5
2. DICK THE STARLING. 7
3. RICHARD THE SECOND...................................10
4. VERDANT...20
5. THE WILD DUCKS. 24
6. THE JAY. 29
7. A YOUNG CUCKOO. 33
8. THE TAMING OF OUR PETS. 36
9. BIRDIE. 42
10. ZÖE, THE NUTHATCH. 46

11.	TITMICE. 53
12.	BLANCHE, THE PIGEON. 58
13.	GERBILLES. 61
14.	WATER SHREWS. 66
15.	SQUIRRELS. 69
16.	A MOLE. 72
17.	HARVEST MICE. 75
18.	THE CALIFORNIA MOUSE. 77
19.	SANCHO THE TOAD. 79
20.	ROMAN SNAILS. 81
21.	AN EARWIG MOTHER. 84
22.	THE SACRED BEETLE. 87
23.	SPIDERS. 90
24.	TAME BUTTERFLIES. 95
25.	ANT-LIONS. 98
26.	ROBINS I HAVE KNOWN. 101
27.	ROBERT THE SECOND. 104
28.	FEEDING BIRDS IN SUMMER AND WINTER 108
29.	RAB, MINOR. 112
30.	A VISIT TO JAMRACH. 115
31.	HOW TO OBSERVE NATURE 119

PREFACE TO THE FIFTH EDITION.

TWO short chapters, one describing the life of an Ant-lion, and the other the habits of a tame Toad, were added to the second edition, which was in other respects a reproduction of the first The present edition has been improved by the adoption of a number of illustrations which were designed for the German translation of this book.

INTRODUCTION.

I HAVE often wished I could convey to others a little of the happiness I have enjoyed all through my life in the study of Natural History. During twenty years of variable health, the companionship of the animal world has been my constant solace and delight. To keep my own memory fresh, in the first instance, and afterwards with a distinct intention of repeating my single experiences to others, I have kept notes of whatever has seemed to me worthy of record in the life of my pets. Some of these papers have already appeared in *The Animal World*; the majority are now printed for the first time.

In the following chapters I shall try to have quiet talks with my readers and tell them in a simple way about the many pleasant friendships I have had with animals, birds, and insects. I use the word friendships advisedly, because truly to know and enjoy the society of a pet creature you must make it feel that you are, or wish to be, its friend, one to whom it can always look for food shelter, and solace; it must be at ease and at home with you before its instincts and curious ways will be shown. Sometimes when friends have wished me to see their so-called "pet," some scared animal or poor fluttering bird has been brought, for whom my deepest sympathy has been excited; and yet there may have been perhaps the kindest desire to make the creature happy, food provided in abundance, and a pleasant home; but these alone will not avail. For lack of the quiet gentle treatment which is so requisite, the poor little captive will possibly be miserable, pining for liberty, hating its prison, dreading the visits of its jailor, and so harassed in its terror that in some cases the poor little heart is broken, and in a few hours death is the result. In the following simple sketches of animal, bird, and insect life, I have tried to show how confidence must be gained, and the little wild heart won by quiet and unvarying kindness, and also by the endeavour to imitate as much as possible the natural surroundings of its own life before its capture. I must confess it requires a large fund of patience to tame any wild creature, and it is rarely possible to succeed unless one's efforts begin in its very early days, before it has known the sweets of liberty.

In many cases I have kept a wild animal or bird for a few days to learn something of its ways, possibly to make a drawing of its attitudes or plumage, and then let it go, else nearly all my pets, except imported creatures, have been reared from infancy, an invalid's life and wakefulness making early-morning feeding of young fledglings less difficult than it would have been in many cases, and often have painful hours been made bearable and pleasant by the interest arising from careful observation of the habits and ways of some new pet animal or bird.

I have always strongly maintained that the love of animated nature should be fostered far more than it usually is, and especially in the minds of the young; and that, in fact, we lose an immense amount of enjoyment by passing through life as so many do without a spark of interest in the marvelous world of nature, that book whose pages are ever lying open before us.

The beauties of the country might as well have been left uncreated for all the interest that thousands take in them. Not only town dwellers, who might be excused for their ignorance, but those who live in the midst of fields and woods, often know so little about the

INTRODUCTION. 3

curious creatures in fur and feathers that exist around them that they are surprised when told the simplest facts about these, their near neighbours.

One reason may be, that it is now so much the fashion to spend the year in various places, and those always moving about have neither the time nor opportunity to cultivate the little undergrowths of quiet pleasures which spring out of a settled home in the country, with its well-tended garden and farmyard, greenhouses, stable, and fields the horses and cattle, petted and kindly cared for from their birth, dogs and poultry, and all kinds of special favourites.

There is a healthy, happy tone about such a life, and where it exists and is rightly maintained, good influence is, or ought to be, felt in and around the home. Almost all children have a natural love of living creatures, and if they are told interesting facts about them they soon become ardent naturalists. I well remember that in my childhood I had a great dread of toads and frogs, and a relative, to whom I owe much for having directed my mind into the love of animated nature, took up a frog in her hand and made me look at the beautiful gold circle round its eyes, its curious webbed feet, its leaping power arising from the long hind legs; she told me also of its wonderful tongue, so long and flexible that it folded back in its mouth, and that the frog would sit at the edge of an ant-hill and throwing out the tongue with its sticky point, would pick off the ants one by one as they came out. When I learnt all this, I began to watch such a curious reptile; my fears vanished, and like Kingsley's little daughter, who had been wisely led to care for all living things and came running to show her father a "dear delightful worm" she had found! so I, too, have been led all through my life to regard every created thing, great or small, attractive or otherwise, as an object well worth the most reverent study.

Perhaps I ought to explain that I have described methods of taming, feeding, and housing one's pets with extreme minuteness in order to help those of my readers who may be very fond of live creatures, and yet from lack of opportunity may have gained no knowledge of their mode of life, and what is required to keep them happily in health and vigour. I have had to learn by experience that attention to very small details is the road to success in keeping pets as well as in other things, and the desire to pass on that experience must be my excuse to more scientific readers for seeming triviality.

Many admirable books have been written by those well qualified to impart their knowledge in every branch of Natural History, and the more such books are read the better, but the following pages simply contain the life histories of my pets and what I personally have observed about them. I shall be glad indeed if they supply any useful information, or lead others to the more careful study of the common every-day things around them with a view to more kindness being shown to all living creatures, and tender consideration for them. I trust I may feel that this little book will then have attained its purpose. May it especially tend to lead the young to see how this beautiful world is full of wonders of every kind, full of evidences of the Great Creator's wisdom and skill in adapting each created thing to its special purpose, and from the whole realm of nature may they be taught lessons in parables, and their hearts be led upward to God Himself, who made all things to reflect His own perfection and glory.

> "Gem, flower, and fish, the bird, the brute,
>   Of every kind occult or known
> (Each exquisitely form'd to suit
>   Its humble lot, and that alone),
> Through ocean, earth, and air fulfil
> Unconsciously their Maker's will."
>
> ELIZA BRIGHTWEN.

REARING BIRDS FROM THE NEST.

THE most delightful of all pets are the birds one has taken the pains to rear from the nest; they never miss the freedom of outdoor life, they hardly know what fear is, they become devotedly attached to the one who feeds and educates them, and all their winsome ways seem developed by the love and care which is given to them.

I strongly deprecate a whole nest being taken; one would not willingly give the happy little parent birds the distress of finding an empty home. After all their trouble in building, laying, sitting, and hatching, surely they deserve the reward of bringing up their little babes.

Too often when boys thus take a nest they simply let the young birds starve to death from ignorance as to their proper food and not rising early enough to feed them.

It is a different matter if, out of a family of six, one takes two to bring up by hand the labour of the old birds is lightened, and four fledglings will sufficiently reward their toil.

The birds should be taken before they are really feathered, just when the young quills begin to show, as at that stage they will not notice the change in their diet and manner of feeding. They need to be carefully protected from cold, kept at first in a covered basket in flannel, and if the weather is cold they should be near a fire, as they miss the warmth of the mother bird, especially at night.

I confess it involves a good deal of trouble to undertake the care of these helpless little creatures. They should be fed every half-hour, from four in the morning until late in the evening, and that for many weeks until they are able to feed themselves.

The kind of food varies according to the bird we desire to bring up, and it requires care to make sure that it is not too dry or too moist, and that it has not become sour, or it will soon prove fatal, for young birds have not the sense of older ones they take blindly whatever is given them.

DICK THE STARLING.

FEW people would think a cat could possibly be a tender nurse to young birds! but such was really the case with a very interesting bird I possessed some years ago.

A young starling was brought up from the nest by the kind care of our cook and the cat! Both were equally sympathetic, and pitied the little unfledged creature, who was by some accident left motherless in his early youth. Cook used to get up at some unheard-of hour in the morning to feed her clamorous pet, and then would bring him down with her at breakfast-time and consign him to pussy's care; she, receiving him with a gentle purr of delight, would let him nestle into her soft fur for warmth.

As Dick became feathered, he was allowed the run of the house and garden, and used to spend an hour or so on the lawn, digging his beak into the turf, seeking for worms and grubs, and when tired he would fly in at the open window and career about until he could perch on my shoulder, or go in search of his two foster-mothers in the kitchen.

His education was carried on with such success that he could soon speak a few words very clearly. Strangers used to be rather startled by a weird-looking bird flying in from the garden, and saying, "Beauty dear, puss, puss, miaow!" But it was still more strange to see Dick sitting on the cat's back and addressing his endearments to her in the above words. Pussy would allow him to investigate her fur with exemplary patience, only objecting to his inquisitive beak being applied to her eyelids to prize them open when she was enjoying her afternoon nap. Dick's love of water led him to bathe in most inconvenient places. One morning, when I returned to the dining-room after a few minutes' absence, I found him taking headers into a glass filter and scattering the contents on the sideboard. After dinner, too, he would dive into the finger-glasses with the same intention, and when hindered in that design would visit the dessert dishes in succession, stopping with an emphatic "Beauty dear!" at the sight of some coveted dainty, to which he would forthwith help himself liberally.

In summer Dick had to resist considerable temptation from wild birds of his own kind, who evidently made matrimonial overtures to him, but though he "camped out" for a few nights now and then, he never seemed to find a mate to his mind, and elected to remain a bachelor and enjoy our society instead of that of his own kith and kin.

Dick was certainly a pattern of industrious activity, never still for two minutes. He seemed haunted by the idea that caterpillars and grubs existed all over the house, and his search for them was carried on under all possible circumstances every plait of one's dress, every button-hole, would be inquired into by his prying little beak in case some choice morsel might chance to be lurking there. Dick lived for a few happy years, and then his bathing propensities most unhappily led to his untimely death. One severely cold day in winter he was missed and searched for everywhere, and after some hours his poor little body was found stiff and cold in a water-tank in the stable-yard, where the ice had been broken. He had as usual plunged in for a bath, and we can only suppose the intense cold had caused an attack of cramp, so that he could not get out again, and thus was drowned. Many tears were shed for the loss of the cheery little bird, who seemed like a bright ubiquitous sunbeam about the house, and our only consolation was the thought that, as far as we knew, he had never had a sorrow in his life, and we can only hope that if there are "happy hunting-grounds" for birds our Dick may be there, bright and happy still

FLYING STARLINGS.

RICHARD THE SECOND

ON a wet stormy day in May a young unfledged bird was blown out of its nest and was picked up in a paved yard where, somehow, it had fallen unhurt.

There he was found by my kind-hearted butler, who appeared with the little shivering thing in his hand to see if I would adopt it The butler pleaded for it, and it squawked its own petition piteously enough, but I was far from strong, and I knew at what very early hours these young feathered people required to be fed. I therefore felt I ought hardly to give up the time which sometimes brought me the precious boon of sleep after a wakeful night. Very reluctantly I refused the gift, and felt wretchedly hard-hearted in doing so. I will confide to my readers that in my secret heart I thought the poor orphan was a blackbird or thrush, and they are birds I feel ought never to be caged; they pine and look so sadly longing for liberty; even their song has a minor key of plaintiveness when it comes through prison bars, and this feeling helped my decision.

A few days after I heard that the birdie was adopted in the pantry, and was being fed "in the intervals of business." When a few days later I was definitely informed that the birdie waif was a starling, then I confess I did begin to long for another little friend such as my former "Dick" had been, and it ended in my receiving Richard the Second, as we called him for distinction, into my own care and keeping, and month after month I was his much-enduring mother. Most fledglings are much the same at firs; whenever I came in sight the gaping beak was ever ready for food, and the capacity for receiving it was wonderful Richard grew very fast; little quills appeared and opened out into feathers; his walking powers increased till he could make a tottering run upon the carpet; and then he began to object to his basket and would have a perch like a grown-up bird, practised going to sleep on one leg, which for a long time was a downright failure and ended in constant tumbles.

He was always out of his cage whilst I was dressing, and was full of fun and play, scheming to get his bath before I did, and running off with anything he could carry. When he was about two months old I had to go to Buxton for a month's visit and decided that I could not leave Richard behind, as he needed constant feeding with little pieces of raw meat and was just old enough to miss my training and care. He was therefore to make his first start as a traveller, in a small cage, papered round the sides, the top being left open for light and air. He was wonderfully brave and good, very observant of everything, and if scared a word from me would reassure him, until at last even an express train dashing past did not make him start. It was very amusing to see the attention bestowed upon him at the various stations where we had to get out. A little crowd would gather round and stare at such a self-possessed small bird. I was asked "if it was a very rare bird?" It seemed almost absurd to have to reply, "No, only a common starling;" but people are so accustomed to see a caged pet flutter in terror at its unusual surroundings, that my kingly Richard rather puzzled his admirers.

When we began life in our apartments, one important consideration in the day's proceedings was the starling's food. There was no home larder to fall back upon, so a daily portion of tender rumpsteak had to be obtained, to the great amusement of the butcher with whom we dealt for our own joints.

About this time the plain grey plumage began to be varied by two patches of brilliant little purple feathers, tipped with greyish-white, which appeared on each side of his breast. Some began to peep out of his back and head. He moulted his tail, and had rich, dark feathers all over, in time, till he arrived at being what he was often called, "a perfect beauty" glossy and brilliant, bronze gold and purple, with reflets of rich green, and little specks of greyish-white all over his breast; this richness of colour, combined with his beautiful sleek shape, made Richard a very attractive bird.

When we returned from Buxton, I was so confident of the bird's tameness I used to carry him in my hand out to the tulip tree, and there I often sat and read, while Richard would pry into the moss and the bark of the tree, searching for insects, and though he could fly well by this time, he did not try to do so, but seemed content to keep near me.

One morning I heard his first articulate word, "Beauty," spoken so clearly it quite startled me. I had been diligently teaching him, by constant repetition, for many weeks, and by degrees he gained the power of speaking one word after another, till at last he was able to say, "Little beauty," "'Ow de doo?" "Pretty, pretty," "Beauty, dear," "Puss, puss," "Miaow," and imitated kissing exactly. All this was intermingled with his native whistle and sundry inarticulate sounds, intended, I suppose, to result in words and sentences some day. Whilst talking and singing, his head was held very upright, and his wings flapped incessantly against his sides, after the manner of the wild birds.

Nothing stirred my indignation more keenly than the question so often asked, "Have you had your starling's tongue slit to make him talk so well?" I beg emphatically to entreat all my readers to do their utmost to put an end to this cruel and perfectly useless custom. My bird's talking powers were remarkable, but they were the result of his intelligence being drawn out and cultivated by constant, loving care, attention to his little wants, and being talked to and played with, and made into a little feathered friend of the family.

Now must be told an episode which cost me no little heartache. Richard was out in my room one morning as usual, when the room door happening to be open, away he flew into the next room, and out at an open window into the garden. I saw him alight on a tree, but by the time I could reach the garden he had gone. I saw a group of starlings in a beech tree near by, and another set were chattering on the house roof, but there was no telling if my Richard was one of them. I called till I was tired, and continued to do so at intervals all day, but no wanderer appeared. His cage had been put on the lawn, but to no purpose. I feared I should never see my pet again, because I supposed he might be lured by the wild birds till he got out of hearing of any familiar voice. I confess it was hard to think of my bright young birdie starving under some hedge, for I felt sure he was too much of a gentleman from his artificial bringing-up to be able to earn his own living. All I could do was to resolve to be up very early next day, and call again and again, on the chance of his being within hearing. Before six o'clock next morning I was seeking the truant. Plenty of wild birds were about, the bright sun glancing on their sleek coats all looking so like my pet it was impossible to distinguish him. I little knew that he was then starving and miserable under a bush in the upper part of the garden. I continued calling and seeking him until breakfast-time, and fast losing all hope of ever seeing him again. About eleven o'clock I was returning from the kitchen garden, with my hands full of fruit and flowers, when, to my intense delight, poor little Richard came slowly out from under a laurel, and stood in the path before me, as veritable a type of a birdish prodigal son as could well be imagined.

His feathers were ruffled, his wings drooping, his whole aspect irresistibly reminded one of the Jackdaw of Rheims; and the way he sidled up to me, with half-closed eyes and drooping head, was one of the most pathetic things I ever experienced. He so plainly said,

"I'm very sorry hope you'll forgive me; won't do it again"; and certainly his mute appeal was not in vain, for down went my fruit and flowers, and with loving words I took up my lost darling, and cooed over him all sorts of affectionate rubbish until we reached home and he was restored to his cage. There his one desire was water. Poor fellow! he was nearly famished. I think another hour would have seen his end. There is no water in the garden, except in the stone vase in front of the dining-room window, and he would not have known how to find that, so he must have been twenty-eight hours without drinking anything beyond a possible drop of dew now and then. I had to feed him with great care a little food, and very often, until he recovered a measure of strength. He was very drooping all day, and I quite feared he might not live after all, he was so nearly starved to death. After some days however, "Richard was himself again," and as bright and amusing as ever. I have not related the amusing characteristics of his "daily tub." His love of water was a perfect passion, and water he would have. At first he was treated to a large glass dish on the matting in the dining-room, but he sent up such a perfect fountain of spray over curtains, couch, and chairs, that the housemaid voted "that bird" a nuisance, and a better plan was devised. In the conservatory is a pool of water, with rock-work and ferns at the back, and there is a central tube where a fountain can be turned on. I made a small island of green moss a little above the water, and, placing Richard upon it, I turned the fountain on to play a delicate shower of spray over him. He was perfectly enchanted, and fluttered, turned about, and frisked, like a bird possessed. As he became accustomed to it, I began to throw handfuls of water over him, and that he did enjoy. He would cower down, and lie with his wings expanded and beak open, receiving charge after charge of water till quite out of breath; then he would run a few paces away on his island till he recovered himself, and then would go back and place himself ready for a renewed douche. I never saw such a plucky bird. If I had been trying to drown him I could not have done more, for sometimes he was knocked backwards into the pool; but no matter, he was up again, and all ready in a minute. He generally tired me out, and when I turned off the fountain, he would either fly or run after me into the drawing-room and go into his cage, which always stood there; and there followed a very careful toilette a general oiling and pluming and fluttering, until his bonnie little feathers were all in good order; and then would follow endless chatter, and he would inform the world that he was a "little beauty," "pretty little dear," &c.

Starlings seem to have an abundant supply of natural oil in the gland where it is stored, for his feathers were never really much wetted by his tremendous baths, and he was a slippery fellow to hold, his plumage was so glossy and sleek.

A word must be said about his temper; it was decidedly not meek by any means, and his will was strong, so the least thing would bring a shower of pecks in token of disapproval, and if scolded his attitude was most absurd; he would draw himself up to a wonderful height, set up his crest feathers, and stand ready to meet all comers, like a little righting cock; and when a finger was pointed at him he would scold and peck, and flap with his wings with the utmost fury; and yet if a kind word was said all his wrath vanished, and he would come on your hand and prize your fingers apart, looking for grubs as usual. It seemed strange that his habit of thus searching for insects everywhere should continue, though he was never by any chance rewarded by finding one. A starling's range of ideas may be summed up in the word "Grubs." It was always immensely amusing to strangers to see Richard, when out in the room, searching with his inquisitive beak in the most hopeless places with a cheerful happy activity, as if he always felt sure that long-looked-for grub, for which he had searched all the years of his life, must be close by, round the corners somewhere, under the penwiper, behind that book, amongst these coloured silks; and if interfered with he would give a peck and a chirp, as much as to say, "Do let me alone, I'm busy; I've got my living to get, and grubs seem scarce." Richard was the only bird I have ever had who learnt the nature of windows, he never flew against them; he had one or two severe concussions, and being a very sensible bird he "concluded" he wouldn't do it again; he would fly backwards and forwards in the drawing-room in swift flight, but I never feared either the windows or the fire, as he avoided both.

Several times Master Richard was found flying about in the drawing-room, and yet no one had let him out; we could only suppose that by some mischance the door must have been left open; yet we all felt morally certain it had been fastened properly, and there was much puzzlement about the matter.

However, the mystery was soon solved by my watching Richard's proceedings. I heard a prolonged hammering and found he was at work upon the hasp of his cage door. He managed to raise it up higher and higher, till by a well-directed peck he sent it clear out of the loop of wire which held it in its place. Still the door was shut, and it required a good many more pecks to force it open, but he succeeded in time, and out he flew delighted to find himself entirely master of the situation. Then I watched with much amusement his deliberate survey of the room.

I was ill at the time, and he first flew to greet me and talk a little; he hopped upon my hand, and holding firmly on my forefinger he went through his usual morning toilette, first an application to his oil gland, then he touched up all his plumage, drew out his wing and tail feathers, fluttered himself into shape, and when quite in order he began to examine the contents of my breakfast tray; took a little sugar, looked to see if there were any grubs under the tray cloth, peered into the cream jug, decided that he didn't like the salt, gave me two or three hard pecks to express his profound affection, and then went off on a voyage of discovery, *autour de ma chambre*. He squeezed himself between every ornament on the mantle-piece, flew to the drawers, and found there some grapes which were very much to his taste; so he was busy for some time helping himself. He visited every piece of furniture, threw down all the little items that he could lift, and, as I was reading, I did not particularly notice what he was about, until he came on a small table near my bed, and then I heard a suspicious noise, and turned to find the indefatigable bird with his beak in my ink bottle, and the sheet already plentifully bespattered with black splashes and little streams of ink trickling over the table cover; such misplaced zeal was not to be borne, so Richard had to be caged. When he was seven months old, his beak began to turn from black to yellow. The colour began to show first at the base of the beak, and it went on gradually, until in a month's time it was nearly all yellow, though it was black at the tip for some time longer. As time went on, Richard's talking powers increased; he quite upset any grave conversation that might be going on; his voice dropped at times to a sort of stage whisper, as if he wished to convey some profound secrets. "Oh, you little beauty, pretty little dear, 'ow de doo?" used to mingle most absurdly with the conversation of his elders and betters. When he could not have his bath in the conservatory, I used still to to give him his glass dish, which we used together, for he would never enjoy his ablutions without me, and I became considerably sprinkled in the process. His delight was to have a water fight, pecking at my fingers, scolding, as if in a great rage, using his claws, and all the while calling me "Dear little Dicky; beauty; pretty little dear," &c., for he had no harder words to scold with; certainly the effect was most comical. When he supposed he had gained the victory, he would settle down to a regular bathe, fluttering and taking headers until he was dripping wet and delightfully happy, and the next thing would be to perch on one's chair, and shake a regular shower of drops over one's books or work.

Richard was not, as a rule, at all frightened by noises, or by being carried about in his cage in strange places, but early one morning, when he was out in my room, he flew away from the window with a piercing scream of terror, and hid himself quite in the dark, behind my pillow, shivering with fright, as if he felt his last hour had come. We found out, when this had occurred several times, that his *bête noire* was a great heron, which used occasionally to leave the lake, and circle round the house, high up in the air. It could only have been by pure instinct that Richard was inspired with such terror whenever he saw the great winged bird, and it showed that artificial training, though it develops additional powers and habits, in no way interferes with natural instinct

The starling has a remarkably active brain; its quickness of movement, swift flight, and never-tiring activity, all show the working of its inner mind; but more than that, it seems to be capable of something akin to reasoning. Richard sometimes dropped a piece of meat on his sanded floor, and I have often seen him take it up and well rinse it in his water, till the sand was cleansed away, and then he would swallow it; and a dry piece of meat he would moisten in the same way. Now this involved a good deal of mental intuition, and I often wondered whether he found out that water would remove the sand by accident, or by a process of thought; in either case, it showed cleverness and adaptability. So also with the processes of opening the door of his cage. He had first to prize up the latch with his beak to a certain height. and then by sudden sharp pecks send it clear of the hasp; then descend to the floor, and by straight pecks send the door open. If he could not get the door to open thus, he understood at once that the latch was not clear of the hasp, so he went back to his perch and pecked at it until he saw it fall down, and then he knew all was right

When the second summer of Richard's life came round, some young starlings were obtained, as we much wished to rear a hen as a mate for Richard in the following year. These birds were placed in a cage in the same room with him, as we hoped he would prove their tutor, and save us the trouble of teaching them. But no; Richard evidently felt profoundly jealous of these intruders, and day after day remained perfectly dumb and out of temper. This went on for a week, and then fearing he might lose his talking powers, I was obliged to remove them and pay special attention to him, to soothe his ruffled feelings. He did not begin to talk until more than a week had passed by, evidently resolving to mark in this way his extreme displeasure at others being admitted to share our friendship a curious instance of innate jealousy in a bird's mind.

For more than five years Richard was a source of constant pleasure and amusement, and was so much a part of my home-life that when anything unusual happened, in the way of a garden-party or a change in daily events from any cause, one's first thought was to provide for his comfort being undisturbed. I confess I dreaded the thought of his growing old, and could not bear to look on to the time when I must learn to do without his sweet, cheering little voice and pleasant companionship. Alas! that time has come, and I must now tell how the little life was quenched.

In a room to which he had access, there was a small aquarium half-full of water thickly covered with pond-weed. "I had left Richard to have his usual bath whilst I went down to breakfast, and when I returned I could nowhere find my pet His usual bath was unused; I called and searched, and at last in the adjoining room I saw the little motionless body floating in the aquarium. The temptation had been too strong; Richard thought to have a lovely bathe, had flown down into the water, no doubt his claws were hopelessly entangled in the weed and thus, as was the case with my former starling Dick, the intense love of bathing led to a fatal end.

The sorrow one feels for the loss of a pet so interwoven with one's life is very real; many may smile at it and call it weakness, but true lovers of animals and birds will know what a blank is felt and how intensely I shall ever regret the untimely fate of my much-loved little Richard.

VERDANT.

ONE day in early summer I found on a gravel walk a poor little unfledged birdie, sitting calmly looking up into the air, as if he hoped that some help would come to him, some pitying hand and heart have compassion upon his desolate condition.

I carried him indoors, and "mothered" the little helpless thing as well as I could, by feeding him with hard-boiled yolk of egg mixed with brown bread and water. Being a hard-billed bird, I supposed that would be suitable food, and certainly he throve upon it. The little blue quills began to tell of coming feathers, his vigorous chirpings betokened plenty of vocal power, and in due time he grew into a young greenfinch of the most irrepressible and enterprising character. His lovely hues of green and yellow led to the name of Verdant being bestowed upon him, and his early experiences made it a somewhat suitable name.

Poor little man! he had no parents to instruct him, and he consequently got into all manner of scrapes. He only learnt the nature of windows and looking-glasses by bitter experience; flying against them with great force, he was often taken up for dead; but his solid little skull resisted all these concussions, and by pouring cold water upon his head and some down his throat, he always managed to recover. He once overbalanced into a bath, and was nearly drowned; he fell behind a wardrobe, and was nearly suffocated; later on he almost squeezed himself to death between the bars of his cage in fact, he had endless escapes of various kinds. He was very amusing in his early youth. Whilst I was dressing he would delight in picking up my scissors, pins, button-hook, and anything else he could lift, and would carry them to the edge of the dressing-table and throw them down, turning his sly little head to see where they had fallen. He delighted in mischief, and was ever on the watch to carry off or misplace things; and yet he was a winning little pet, fearless in his confidence, perching on one's head or shoulder, and hindering all dressing operations by calmly placing his little body in the way, regardless of consequences.

He lived in his cage during the day, and next to him, on the same table, lived a bullfinch a very handsome bird, but heavy and lethargic to a degree; he sang exquisitely, and for that gift I suppose Verdant admired him, for his delight was to be as near him as possible. Perched on the top of his cage, he gazed down at his friend, and in great measure imitated his singing. Bully, on the contrary, hated Verdant, and would have nothing to do with him. The two characters were a great source of amusement to us.

Verdant was always let out at meal-times to fly about and enjoy his liberty, and I am sorry to say he was always on the look-out for any mischief that might be possible. Bully's water-jar was fastened outside by a small pin; this Verdant discovered was movable, and before long we were startled by the fall of the said water-jar, the greefinch having pulled out the pin; he then began upon the seed-box, and that also fell, to his great delight; he was then talked to and scolded, and up went his pretty yellow wings with angry flappings, and his open beak scolded back again in the most hardened manner. He was greatly interested in watching the numerous birds frequenting a basket filled with fat which hung outside the window, and he would swing backwards and forwards on the tassel of the blind, chirping to the outsiders, and watching all their little squabbles. Sunflower seeds were his greatest dainty; he would perch upon the hand to receive one, or if it were held between the lips he would flutter and poise upon the wing to take it. A sort of swing with a chain and movable wheel was provided, upon which Verdant soon learned to perch and swing, whilst he amused himself by pecking at the chain till he disengaged the sunflower seeds I had fixed in the links. When he was more than a year old, and I thought he might be depended upon, I tried the rather anxious experiment of letting him out of doors. He soon became quietly happy, investigating the wonders of tree branches, inquiring into the taste of leaves and all kind of novelties, when two or three sparrows flew at him and scared him considerably. Away he went, followed by the sparrows, and I began to repent my experiment, and feared he might go beyond my ken and lose himself. He was out nearly an hour, but at last he returned and went quietly into his cage. It seemed strange that the wild birds should so soon discover that he was not one of their clique, but I suppose Verdant revealed the secret by looking frightened, and the others could not resist the fun of chasing him. For more than a year and a half my birdie was a constant pleasure. Whenever he entered the dining-room my first act was to open Verdant's cage, when he would always fly to the bullfinch's cage and greet him with a chirp, then look to see if his friend had any provender that he could get at a piece of lettuce between the bars, or a spray of millet to which he could help himself; no matter that Bully remonstrated with open beak, Verdant calmly feasted on stolen goods con gusto, and then scouted around for any dainties on the carpet, where he sometimes found a stray sunflower seed, always his greatest delight. After his summer moulting he became wonderfully vigorous, and would fly round the room with such velocity that I often felt afraid he might some day fly against the plate-glass windows and injure himself.

That mournful day came at last! He had been out as usual at breakfast-time, came on my finger for a seed, had his bath, and went on the little swing for more seeds, and flew about with all his joyous life and vigour. We had only left the room for a few moments, when, on returning, the dear little bird lay dead beneath the window, against which he had flown with such force as to break his neck and cause instant death.

The sorrow of that moment will never be forgotten; indeed, I cannot even now think of my little pet with undimmed eyes he was a moment before so full of life and beauty, so fearless, such a "sonsie" little fellow; and then to hold the little golden green body in my hand and watch the fast-glazing eye, and think that I should never again have my cheery little friend to greet me and be glad at my coming, was one of those sharp pangs that true lovers of nature alone can understand. From all such I know I shall have sympathy in the tragic death of my much-loved little Verdant

WILD DUCK.

THE WILD DUCKS.

HEN our grass was being cut the mowers came upon a wild duck's nest containing eight eggs; they were carried whilst still warm and placed under a sitting hen; in a week's time she brought out eight fluffy little ducklings, which were placed with her under a coop in the farmyard. I paid them a visit the next day, but, alas! I saw four little corpses lying about in the grass, the remaining four were chirping piteously, and the hen was in despair at being unable to comfort her uncanny children. Evidently their diet was in fault; I thought I would take them in hand, and therefore had the coop brought round to the garden, and placed under the drooping boughs of a deodar near the drawing-room window, where I could watch over them.

I gave the wee birdies a pan of water, and placed in it some finely-shred lettuce, with grits and brown bread crumbs, not forgetting suitable food for the poor distracted hen. It was charming to hear the little happy twitterings of the downy babes, how they gobbled and sputtered and talked to each other over their repast, swimming to and fro as if they had been ducks of mature age and experience, instead of mere yellow fluffs of a day old; and, finally, they seemed to remember they had a warm, comfortable mother somewhere, and sought refuge under her kindly wings, where I left them exchanging confidences in little drowsy chirps.

I found it needful to guard my little brood with fine wire-work, for some carrion crows kept hovering near, and a weasel was constantly on the watch to carry them off; but these enemies were successfully baffled, and three of the ducks survived all dangers and grew to beautiful maturity, the fourth having died in infancy from an accidental peck from the hen. In rearing all wild creatures the great thing is to study and imitate, as nearly as possible, their natural surroundings, and especially their diet. Chopped lettuce and worms made a fair substitute for their natural food, but the jubilation that went on when a mass of water-weed, full of insects, water snails, &c., was brought them, showed that they knew by instinct what suited them best. With constant care and attention they grew very tame, and would eat out of one's hand, and when let out of the coop would follow me to a certain heap of dead leaves where worms abounded, and there, with the most amusing eagerness, they pounced upon their wriggling prey, snatching the worms out of each others beak, and tumbling over one another in their excitement, all the while making a special chirp of exceeding happiness.

They were named Tiny, Sir Francis Drake, and Luther I fear the last name had a covert allusion to the "Diet of Worms."

When the purple feathers began to show in their wings, and they considered themselves quite too old to pay any allegiance to their hen-mother, they began to absent themselves for some hours each afternoon, and this, too, in a most secret fashion, for I could never tell how they disappeared, but they returned in due time, walking quietly in Indian file, and lay down in their coop. At last I traced them to a pond a long distance off it really seemed as if they had scented the water, for they had to traverse a lawn and wood, go across a drive, and through a hedge and field, and then the pond was in a hollow where they could not possibly have seen it; but there I found my little friends in high glee, darting over the surface of the water, splashing, diving, sending up showers of spray from their wings, and going on as if they were possessed. I called to them, and in a moment they quieted down, and behaved exactly as children would have done when caught tripping they came out of the water and followed me, in the meekest and most penitent manner, back to their home under the deodar.

These birds would stay the whole morning with me in perfect content if they were allowed to nestle into a wool mat placed at the doorstep of the French window leading out upon the lawn; there they would plume themselves and sometimes preen each other, and I could watch the way in which the feathers were drawn through the apparently awkward bill, yet I suppose so suited for its various uses; anyway the feathers came out from its manipulations as smooth and sleek as velvet, and when the toilet was over the head found its rest behind the wing, and profound sleep followed. Sometimes my friends would make a spring upon the sofa by my side, I fear with a view to forthcoming worms, of which they well knew I was the purveyor; and nothing could exceed the slyness of their eyes as they looked up at me and mutely suggested an expedition to that heap of leaves!

I must say I derived an immense amount of amusement from those ducks; they had such innate character of their own, quite unlike any other bird I ever came across.

I had often looked forward to the time when they would take to their wings and come down upon the lawn from aerial heights with a grand fuss and fluttering of wings, but that desire they never gratified. The day came at last when I saw them circling high up in the air, so high that they were mere specks in the sky, but where they alighted I never could find out. They always re-appeared, walking solemnly (the little hypocrites!) one after the other, as if they had been doing nothing in particular, and were now coming in exemplary fashion to be fed. I believe it is very rarely the case that wild ducks, however they may appear domesticated, will remain all the year through with those who have reared them, and really take their place in the poultry-yard with the other inmates. Still it has been known, and I will subjoin an account given me by a friend, which goes to prove that such a state of things is possible. My friend gave me in substance the following account of her wild ducks:—

"There are different kinds of wild ducks; these are mallards. The first we had were hatched by hens. They feed with the other ducks, but show a decided preference for Indian corn. They are very troublesome about laying, often leaving their eggs exposed, where the crows find them and carry them off. We gather most of them we find, to take care of them (though the ducks lay in different places each time their nest is robbed) until there are preparations for sitting, when, if we have been fortunate enough to discover the fact, we add a number of the previously gathered eggs."

"The sitting duck comes for food every two or three days, and that is all we see of her for some time, until at length she may be seen coming through the meadow, the half-grown mowing grass behind her trembling and waving in an unusual manner: by-and-by, the road or shorter grass is reached, when it is found the proud mother is bringing home her little fluffy family of perhaps eight to eleven darkie ducklings quick, active, tiny things that refuse at first all friendly advances, but becoming accustomed to their surroundings soon behave much in the manner of their elders. There are dreadful fights on the pond when two or more little families arrive about the same time, the mother of one flock tyrannizing over the members of another, and thus causing many deaths. They often fly away, but they always come back again. All through the winter they go under cover with the other ducks, but when spring comes they are not to be found at night; nevertheless they are sure to be ready for breakfast next morning."

I confess I always had a faint hope that my ducks might stay with me, or at any rate return from time to time, but their wild nature prevailed, and they finally left; only Luther reappeared alone one day and took his last "diet" from my hand; but there was a look in his pretty blue eye which said plainly, "You will never see me again," and he had his final caress and departed "to fresh woods and pastures new."

THE JAY.

MY Jay was taken from the parent nest, built on the stem of an ivy-covered tree which had been blown down in the winter. A young jay is a curious-looking creature: the exquisite blue wing feathers begin to show before the others are more than quills; the eyes are large and bright blue, and when the great beak opens it shows a large throat of deepest carmine, so that it possesses the beauty of colour from its earliest days, and when full grown and in fine plumage it is one of the handsomest of our birds. In its babyhood my jay was much like other young things of his kind, always clamouring for food, and seeming to care for little else, but as he grew up he attached himself to me with a wonderful strength of affection which entirely reversed this order of things, for whenever I came into the room he was restless and unhappy until I came near enough for him to feed me, he would look carefully into his food-trough, and at last select what he thought the most tempting morsel, and then put it through the bars of his cage into my mouth. He would sometimes feed other people, but as a rule he disliked strangers, and I have known him even take water in his beak and squirt it at those who displeased him. On the whole, a jay is not a very desirable pet; he is restless in a cage, and too large to be quite convenient when loose in a room; again, his great timidity is a drawback the least noise, the sight of a cat or dog, puts him in a nervous fright, and he flutters about with anxious notes of alarm. He is seen to best advantage hopping about on a lawn, where he may be attracted by acorns being strewn in winter and spring. It is a pity that his marauding habits in game preserves lead to his being so ruthlessly shot by gamekeepers till it is almost a rare sight to see the handsome bird and hear his note of alarm in the woods. One morning I saw a jay on the lawn near the house, and rather wondering as to what he was seeking, in a minute or two I saw him pounce upon a young half-fledged bird and carry it off in his beak, a helpless little baby wing fluttering in the air as he flew away. Their sight is wonderfully keen, and their cunning is amusing to watch as they steal by careful steps nearer and nearer to their prey, and at last by a sudden dart secure it and make off in rapid flight.

After a year or two my poor jay met with a very sad fate. A garden-party was to take place, and knowing the jay's terror of any unusual noise or upstir, I carried his cage to a quiet room where I hoped he would be quite happy and hear nothing.

I, however, did not happen to notice that, later on, the band had established their quarters near this room, and I suppose the unwonted sounds drove the poor bird into a wild state of terror, and that in his flutterings he had caught his leg in the bars of the cage; anyway, I went up about the middle of the party to see how my pet

THE JAY.

was faring, when I found him in utter misery clinging to the bars, his thigh dislocated and his leg hopelessly broken. It was a mournful duty to carry him away to merciful hands that would end his torture by an instant death. For many a day I missed that bright, handsome birdie who had always a welcome for me and the offer of such hospitality as his cage afforded.

A YOUNG CUCKOO.

LOOKING out of my window before six o'clock one bright morning in early summer, I chanced to see a large bird sitting quietly on the gravel walk. Its feathers were ruffled as if it felt cold and miserable, and its drooping head told a tale of unhappiness from some cause or other. Whilst I was watching it, a little bird darted with all its force against the larger one, and made it roll over on the path; it slowly rose up again, but in another minute a bird from the other side flew against it and again rolled it over. Such conduct could not be tolerated, so, dressing quickly, I went out, and picking up the strange bird I found it was a young cuckoo nearly starved to death, having, as I supposed, lost its foster-parents. The bird was in beautiful plumage, except down the front of its throat, where the repeated attacks of the small birds in showing their usual enmity towards the cuckoo, had stripped off the feathers. The poor bird was only skin and bone, nearly dying from lack of food and persecution, and made no resistance when I brought him in to see if I could act the part of foster-mother. Finely-mixed raw meat and

A YOUNG CUCKOO.

brown bread seemed to me the best substitute for his insect diet but he was an awkward baby to feed though sinking for want of nourishment he would not open his great beak, and every half-hour he had to be fed sorely against his will with many flapping of his wings and other protests of his bird nature. He would not stay quiet in any sort of cage, but when allowed to perch on the rim of a large basket quite free, he remained happily enough by the hour together. After a few days he grew into a vigorous, active bird, flying round the room, and too wild to be retained with safety. He was therefore let loose, and soon flew quite out of sight. I should hope he was quite able to support himself by his own exertions. I must say he showed no gratitude for my benevolent succour in his time of need.

YOUNG CUCKOO ATTACKED BY BIRDS.

THE TAMING OF OUR PETS.

SINCE the love of animal and bird pets seems so universal, both amongst rich and poor, it is well that the desire to keep creatures in captivity should be wisely directed, and that young people especially should be led to think of the things that are requisite to make their pets live and prosper in some degree of happiness.

I have often been consulted by some sweet, impulsive child about its "pet robin" or "dear little swallow," as to why it did not seem to eat or feel happy? and have found the poor victims quietly starving to death on a diet of oats, canary seed, or even green leaves, the infant mind not feeling quite sure what the "pretty birdies" lived upon.

It is needless to say we might as well try to keep a bird on pebbles as give hard grain to a soft-billed insect-eating bird; but this kind of cruelty is constantly practised simply from ignorance. I would therefore endeavour to give a few general rules for the guidance of those who have a new pet of some kind, which they wish to domesticate and tame.

THE TAMING OF OUR PETS.

To begin with animals; suitable food, a comfortable home, means of cleanliness, and exercise are essential to their health and comfort. These four requisites are seldom fully attended to. Often a large dog is kept in a back yard in London chained up week after week kept alive, it is true, by food and water, but without exercise, and with no means of ridding himself of dirt and insects by a plunge now and then into a pond or river. No wonder his piteous howls disturb the neighbours, and he is spoken of as "that horrid dog!" as if it was his fault poor fellow! that he feels miserable and uses his only language of complaint.

One would suggest, it is better not to keep such a dog in a confined space in town, but if he is to be retained he should have one or two daily scampers for exercise, the opportunity of bathing, if he is a water-dog, plenty of fresh water, dog-biscuits, and a few bones twice a day, and a clean house and straw for bedding.

I would call attention to the piece of solid brimstone so persistently put into dogs' water pans. It is placed there with the best intention, but is utterly useless, seeing it is a perfectly insoluble substance, but a small teaspoonful of powdered brimstone mixed now and then with the water would be lapped up when the animal drinks, and would tend to keep his skin and coat in good condition.

Different animals need treating according to their nature and requirements, and surely it is well to try and find out from some of the many charming books on natural history all the information which is needed to make the new pet happy in its captivity. It is both useless and cruel to try to keep and tame newly caught, full-grown English birds. After being used to their joyous life amongst tree branches, in happy fellowship with others of their own kind, living on food of their own selection, it is hardly likely they can be reconciled to the narrow limits of a cage and the dreariness of a solitary life; it is far better not to attempt keeping them, for what pleasure can there be in seeing the incessant flutterings of a miserable little creature that we know is breaking its heart in longings for liberty, and though it may linger a while is sure to die at last of starvation and sorrow. No, the only way to enjoy friendships with full-grown birds is to tame them by food and kindness, till such a tie of love is formed that they will come into our houses and give us their sweet company willingly.

No cruelty of any kind whatever should be tolerated for a moment in our treatment of the tender dumb creatures our Heavenly Father has given us to be a solace and joy during our life on earth.

The taming of pets requires a good many different qualities much patience, a very quiet manner, and a cheery way of talking to the little creatures we desire to win into friendship with us; it is wonderful how that prevents needless terrors.

There are no secrets that I am aware of in taming anything, but love and gentleness. Directly a bird flutters, one must stop and speak kindly; the human voice has wonderful power over all animated nature, and then try to see what is the cause of alarm, and remove it if possible. In entering a room where your pet is, always speak to it, and by the time you have led it to give an answering chirp, the taming will go on rapidly, because there is an understanding between you, and the little lonely bird feels it has a friend, and takes you instead of its feathered companions, and begins to delight in your company.

A person going silently to a cage and dragging out the bottom tray will frighten any bird into flutterings of alarm, which effectually hinders any taming going on; but approach gently, talking to the bird by name, pull the tray quietly a little way, and then stop and speak, and so draw it out by degrees and the thing is done, and no fright experienced. A better way still is to have a second cage, and let birdie hop into that while you clean the other, and then it is amusing to see the pleasure and curiosity shown on his return when he finds fresh seed, pure water, and some dainty green food supplied; the loud chirpings tell of great delight and satisfaction, and the dreaded process is at last looked forward to as a time of recreation. It is much best that one person only should attend to the needs of a pet; indeed, I doubt if taming can ever go on satisfactorily unless this rule is observed; a bird is perplexed and scared if plans are changed, and, not knowing what is required of him, he grows flurried, and the training of weeks past may be undone in a single day.

Only those who have tried to educate birds can have any idea of the way in which their little minds will respond to affectionate treatment shown in a sensible way. They have a language of their own which we must set ourselves to learn if we would be en rapport with them. Their different chirpings each mean something, and a little observation will soon show what it is; for instance, my canary fairly shrieks when she sees lettuce on the breakfast-table, and her grateful note of thanks when it is bestowed upon her is of quite a different character. So also is her tender little sound of rejoicing when I give her some broken egg-shell; she seems to value it immensely, and chirps to me with a great piece of it in her bill, quite regardless of good manners. I often think with pain how much birds must suffer when hour after hour they call and chirp and entreat for something they want, which they can see and long for, and yet the dull-minded human beings they live with pay no heed to them, food and water are given, but, in many cases, nothing more all day long, not even a little chickweed or groundsel, or the much-needed eggshell to supply strength to their little bones. A bright word or two for birdie now and then, and a few friendly chirps as we enter the room, would do much to cheer the little prisoner's life, and would soon bring a charming response in fluttering wings and evident pleasure at our return.

This state of things cannot be attained in a day or a month; it is only by persistent kindness, exercised patiently, until the little heart is won to a perfect trust in you as a true friend.

Birds can easily be trained to come out for their daily bath, and then go back to their cage of their own accord, but it needs patience at first. The bird must never be caught by the hand or driven about, but if the cage is put on the floor with some nice food in it, and the bird is called and gently guided to it, though it may take an hour to do it the first time, it will at last hop in, and then the door may be

very quietly shut. Next time he will know what you wish and will be much more amenable, until at last it will be the regular thing to go home when the bath is over.

I would condemn the practice of making birds draw up their own water; they are never free to satisfy their thirst without toilsome effort, and are much more liable to accident when chained to an open board than when kept in a cage. It is also sad to know that dozens of birds are starved to death or die of thirst whilst being taught this trick frequently but one out of many is found to have the aptitude to learn it.

It is a great help if some specially favourite food can be discovered by which the pet creature can be rewarded for good conduct. I never take away food or water to induce obedience by privation a practice which I fear is often resorted to in training creatures for public exhibition but an additional dainty I much enjoy to bestow, as a means of winning what is at first, it is true, merely cupboard love, but it soon grows into something far deeper, a lifelong friendship, quite apart from the food question.

Cleanliness is a very important item in a bird's happiness. Whilst kept in a cage with but little sand and an outside water-glass which affords no means of washing its feathers, a bird is apt to become infested with insects; it is tormented by them day and night, and having no means of ridding itself of them, it grows thin and mopy, and at last dies a miserable death.

There should be a bath supplied daily, suited to the size of the bird, and so planned that the cage itself may not get wet, else it may give the bird cramp to have to sit on a damp perch or floor. When its feathers are dry, some insect powder may be carefully dusted under the bird's wings, at the back of his head, where parasites are especially apt to congregate, and all over the body, only taking care that the powder may not get into the bird's eyes. The cage itself should be well washed with carbolic soap and water, all the corners scrubbed with a small brush; and, when dry, it might be sponged with carbolic lotion over the wire-work to kill any insects which may yet remain.

BIRDIE.

AMONGST all the different birds which are kept in cages, either for their beauty or song, there is one which to my mind far excels all others, not only in its vocal powers, which are remarkable but for its very unusual intelligence. I refer to the Virginian nightingale. It is a handsome, crimson-plumaged bird, rather smaller than a starling, not unfrequently seen in bird-sellers' collections, but seen there to the worst possible advantage, for, being extremely shy and sensitive, and taking keen notice of everything around, the slightest voice or movement in the shop will make it flutter against the bars of its cage in an agony of fright, and it therefore looks a most unlikely bird to become an interesting pet; but I will try to show what may be done by gentle kindness to overcome this natural timidity. This will be seen in the history of Birdie, my first Virginian nightingale, my daily companion for fourteen years.

He had belonged to a relative, and there was no way of tracing the age of the bird when first obtained; I can therefore only speak of those years in which he was in my possession. Birdie had been accustomed to live in a cage on a high shelf in the kitchen, well cared for, no doubt, but, untamed and unnoticed, he led a lonely life, and was one of the wildest birds I ever met with. For many months his flutterings, when any one came near his cage, could not be calmed, but by always speaking to him when entering the room, and if possible giving him a few hemp-seeds or any little dainty, he grew to endure one's presence; then, later on, he would begin to greet one with a little clicking note, though still retreating to the furthest corner of the cage, and a year or two passed by before he would take anything out of my hand, but this was attained by offering him his one irresistible temptation, *i.e.*, a lively spider; this he would seize and hold in his beak while he hopped about the cage, clicking loudly with delight. After a time I began to let him out for an hour or two, first releasing him when he was moulting and could not fly very easily. He learned to go back to his cage of his own accord, and was rewarded by always finding some favourite morsel there. Thus, by slow degrees, he lost all fear, and attached himself to me with a strength of affection that expressed itself in many endearing little ways. When called by name he would always answer with a special chirp and look up expectantly, either to receive something or to be let out. His song was very similar to the English nightingale, extremely liquid and melodious, with the same "jug-jug," but more powerful and sustained. On my return to the room after a short absence he would greet me with delight, fluttering his outspread wings and singing his sweetest song, looking intently at me, swaying his head from side to side, and whilst this ecstasy of song lasted he would even refuse to notice his most favourite food, as if he must express his joy before appetite could be gratified. After a few years he seemed to adopt me as a kind of mate! for as spring came round he endeavoured to construct a nest by stealing little twigs out of the grate and flying with them to a chosen retreat behind an ornamental scroll at the top of the looking-glass. He spent a great deal of time fussing about this nest, which never came to anything, but he very obligingly attended to my supposed wants by picking up an occasional fly, or piece of sugar, and, hovering before me on the wing, would endeavour to put it into my mouth; or, if he was in his cage, would mince up a spider or caterpillar with water, and then, with his beak full of the delicious compound, would call and chirp unceasingly until I came near and "made believe" to taste it, and not till then would he be content to enjoy it himself.

During an absence from home, Birdie once escaped out of doors, and was seen on the roof of the house singing in high glee; the servants called him, the cage was put out, but all to no purpose, he evidently meant to have "a real good time," and kept flying from one tree to another until he was a quarter of a mile from home. A faithful servant kept him in sight for three hours, by which time hunger made him return to our garden, where he feasted on some raspberries, took a leisurely bath in a tub of water, and at length flew in at a bedroom window, where he was safely caged. I never knew a bird with so much intelligence, one might almost say reasoning power. He was once very thirsty after being out of his cage for many hours, and at luncheon he went to an empty silver spoon and time after time pretended to drink, looking fixedly at me as if he felt sure I should know what he meant, and waited quietly until I put water into the spoon. Another curious trait was his sense of humour. Whilst I was writing one day he went up to a rose, which was at the far end of the table, and began pecking at the leaves. I told him not to do it, when, to my surprise, he immediately ran the whole length of the table and made a scolding noise up in my face, and then, just like a naughty child, went back and did it again. He would sometimes try to tease me away from my writing by taking hold of my pen and tugging at a corner of the paper, and whenever the terrible operation of cutting his claws had to be gone through, he quietly curled up his toes and held the scissors with his beak, so that it needed two people to circumvent his clever resistance. He had wonderfully acute vision, and would let me know directly a hawk was in sight, though it might be but the merest speck in the sky. He once had a narrow escape, for a sparrow-hawk made a swoop at him in his cage just outside the drawing-room window, and had no one been at hand would probably have dragged him through the bars. Whenever he saw a jay or magpie, a jackdaw or cat, his clicking note always told me of some enemy in sight. For many years Birdie was my cherished pet, never was there a closer friendship. As I passed his cage each night I put my hand in to stroke his feathers, and was always greeted with a low, murmuring note of affection never heard in the daytime.

It was with deep concern that I watched Birdie's declining strength; there was no disease, only weakness, and at last appetite failed, but even then he would take whatever I offered him and hold it in his beak as if to show that even to the last he would try to please me as far as he could, but he wanted nothing but the quiet rest which came at length, and dear little Birdie is now only a cherished memory of true friendship.

ZÖE, THE NUTHATCH.

A VISIT to a bird-dealer's shop always awakens a deep feeling of pity in my mind as I look at the unhappy, flutter little captives, and think of the breezy hillsides and pleasant lanes from which they came, to be shut up in cages a few inches square, with but little light, a stifling atmosphere, strange diet, and no means of washing their ruffled feathers or stretching their wings in flight. Truly, they are in evil case, and no wonder so many die off within a few days of their capture! In some places they are better cared for than in others, but in most bird-shops dirt and misery seem to prevail amongst the tenants of the cages.

One such place I have often visited for the sake of meeting with live curios. The owner was a kind-hearted woman, and did not intentionally ill-treat her live-stock; but the shop was very dark and dirty, and one could but wonder how anything contrived to live in such close, stivy air. On going in one day, I nearly walked over a large, pensive-looking duckling which stood in the middle of the shop. His brother had been considered suitable for the adornment of a table-lamp with a looking-glass stand, on which a bright yellow duckling was placed, as if swimming on water; this bird, having some darker markings, was of no use for that purpose and had been allowed to live. He had a strange, old-fashioned look, and gave one the impression that he was already tired of life and felt bored. A lark on its little piece of turf, fluttering and looking up for a glimpse of blue sky; a dejected robin, with no tail to speak of, and sundry other sad-looking specimens met my pitying gaze, and I suppose I had caught their sorrowful expression, for I was startled by a sharp voice near me, saying, "What's the matter?" I turned to reply, and found the inquiry was made by a grey parrot, who introduced himself as "Pretty Poll," and was ready to make friends to any extent. But my attention had been caught by seeing what looked like a nuthatch: only it was moping and ill, with eyes shut and feathers ruffled. I asked about it, and was told it had some injury to its foot, and was unsaleable, as the woman feared it would not live. I made a bid for it, and it was accepted. I confess I was not sorry to leave the stifling air of the shop and bring my new pet home. I fitted up a large cage with pieces of wood and tree-bark, a pan for bathing, sand, and fine gravel; a bone with a little meat upon it hung from the roof of the cage, and other suitable food was placed in a tin. The poor birdie was a pitiable object for some days; she ate now and then, but remained for the most part quite still, with closed eyes, from morning till night. Then she began to creep up and down the small tree-stem I had placed in the cage. She took a bath and plumed herself, and in less than a fortnight she became quite well and vigorous, and very amusing in a variety of ways. Never was there a more active, busy little creature.

Her characteristic was life, so she was named "Zöe," and before long she seemed to recognize her name, and would give an answering chirp. The pieces of bark appeared to afford a never-failing interest They were examined and investigated in every crevice. Like a little woodpecker hanging head downwards, Zöe would hammer at a nut fixed in the cracks of the bark, and would hide away unfortunate mealworms not required for immediate use.

Zöe regularly honeycombed the little tree-stem with her incessant hammering, and in the numerous holes thus made she kept her supply of food. No sooner was her tin filled with small pieces of raw meat than she began stowing them all away for future use. She seemed to exercise a good deal of thought about the matter; a morsel would be put in and out of a hole half a dozen times before it was considered settled and suitable, and then it had to be well rammed in and fixed, and off went the busy little creature to fetch another piece, and so on, till all was disposed of, and the tin left empty. Zöe was greatly exercised by a half-opened Brazil nut: it was too large to fix into the bark, it would not keep steady while she pecked at it, and yet there were good things inside which must be obtained. I watched her various devices with great amusement. She hung head downwards from the tree-stem and hammered at it on the ground, but it shifted about, and she made no way; then she carried it in her beak and tried fitting it into various places. I hope she did not swear at it, but she seemed to think the thing was possessed, for it was not like the ordinary nuts: she could manage them; they would go into holes in the bark; this wouldn't fit anywhere, and yet she could not give it up. At last, by a bright inspiration, she got it fixed into a space between the tree-stem and the side of the cage. Now she was in high glee, and all the household might have heard the rapping that went on while she scooped out the inside and chipped off pieces to be hidden carefully away in some secret place.

Zöe had a cosy nook under a sloping piece of bark, to which she would retire at times, and sitting down on the bottom of her cage in the shadow, looked like a little grey mouse. When appetite brought her out again, she would go to her tree-larder and pick out the choice hidden morsels, as if they were the insects which would have been her food if her lot had been cast amongst tree-branches instead of in a cage.

When winter began, Zöe was placed in the conservatory, where a tame robin often came for a few hours to enjoy his daily crumbs and the pleasant warmth of the air. Bobby was greatly puzzled at the nuthatch, watched her hammerings from the top of the cage, walked round it, surveying the provisions inside, and at last he made up his mind to get in somehow and partake of the longed-for dainties. I could see quite plainly the attraction, the hesitation, the pros and cons, and then, finally, the resolve, and felt very curious as to how the birdish mind would carry out its intention. There was only one place, where the bars were rather widely apart, so that the nuthatch could have got out if she had possessed half the wits of the robin. After a quiet survey and a few flights backwards and forwards, Bobby saw this place, and made towards it, sat and considered for a few seconds, and finally went in. The nuthatch was sitting quietly under her piece of bark, and did not see him; so he picked up the desired morsels, and, after a few minutes, went out where it came in. These visits he repeated frequently through the day, but once I was amused to see that he forgot "the way out," and put himself in a great fuss, realized that a cage was a prison, and flew up and down in a fright, until by chance he saw the opening, and glided out. At last Zöe caught him in the act of purloining her goodies, and was most indignant. A rush at the thief, with an angry chirp, sent Bobby flying away in ignominious haste, a wiser, but not a repentant bird; for he continued his robberies, only with care to avoid being caught; he ventured only a little way into the cage, ready to go out at a moment's notice.

Zöe had a good deal of quiet humour, and was a character in her way. She considered me very attentively one day, with a roguish look in her black eyes, and then, going to her tree-stem larder, she pulled out a hidden mealworm and held it up for me to see, with an evident wish that I should know about it, and possibly with a little birdish triumph that she possessed such delights; and then it was put back again and well rammed into its crevice until the hungry moment should arrive. After a few months Zöe became tame enough to be let out of her cage, and would hop quietly about the room, and, like a small, grey-coated detective, would peer about stealthily under tables and chairs in search of live dainties; and extremely pretty she looked as she crept up the curtains with jerky motions, evidently thinking they were tree-stems where, by careful search, delightful centipedes and beetles might be found.

I do not know if naturalists have remarked that the nuthatch has a very limited range of vision. Zöe could see nothing beyond twelve or fourteen inches; the most tempting mealworm might lie on the floor of the cage unnoticed if she happened to be on her tree-stem; and I have tried bringing the insect nearer by degrees, and found that only when within a foot of her eyes could she see it, and I fancy then only indistinctly as she would peer about excitedly, as if uncertain what it was, until near enough to be in the focus of clear vision, and then, by a sudden dart, she would seize and flit away with it.

At first Zöe's roosting-place was under the curved piece of bark lying on the floor of her cage, but after a time she took up her nightly quarters in a small box which hooked on to the side of her cage. It was a very cramped and uncomfortable lodging, and I wondered how she contrived to squeeze into such a small space. It occurred to me that a little cocoa-nut with a hole at one end would be the sort of sleeping-chamber she would prefer, as being most like a hole in a tree-stem, in which, probably, nuthatches roost.

An empty cocoa-nut was, therefore, provided. With birdish distrust and caution Zöe only eyed it for some days, then perched on it; but finally she went in, and it was amusing to see her evident delight: how she went incessantly in and out, and turned round and round inside, and finally sat down and remained in it for an hour or more, quite still and happy, peering out at any one passing by, her sleek head and neck looking remarkably like a snake, and her furtive black eye observantly watching all that went on around her.

Her cage, when not in the conservatory, was placed on a table in the drawing-room, close to where I was sitting, and thus she was frequently spoken to and noticed, which is one great secret in taming birds and animals. They soon learn to greet one with some token of recognition, and their often solitary lives are brightened and cheered by such companionship.

An amusing thing occurred one day while I was away from home for a few hours. Zöe's cage had been placed in the sun, and a friend of mine, glancing at the bird, saw her in an apparently dying state, her head hanging on one side, the beak wide open, all the feathers ruffled, and the whole aspect of the bird indicating the near approach of death. The bell was rung, the servants came in, and whispered consultations were held as to what could be done, and "What would mistress say?" seemed the uppermost thought. All at once, Zöe jumped down and began a vigorous hammering at her tree-stem, as full of life as ever, and she was at once voted "a little impostor." When I returned and heard the account, it was easy to explain that my birdie had been enjoying a sun bath, which always gives rise to most lackadaisical positions while the state of dreamy absorption lasts.

The mealworms which Zöe mainly lived upon were kept in a tin biscuit-box, which she knew well by sight, and one day, being too busy to spare time to feed her with them, I opened her cage-door and put the box down a little way from the cage on the floor, and placed a small log of wood for her to descend by. Down she came, perched on the edge of the box, looked at the layers of flannel which covered her delightful worms, and tugged at one corner after another till she obtained her prey. After swallowing two or three, she thought a little store might be useful, and began taking them in her beak, and searching for some convenient hiding-places, but as I did not desire to have the drawing-room neatly ornamented with mealworms, I had to prevent that little design being carried out. My tiny pet lived happily for about a year, but when the moulting time came she grew weak and ill, and did not seem to have strength to produce her new plumage; for, in spite of all possible care, she drooped and died. She lives in my memory as one of the most gentle, innocent birdies I have ever had, absolutely without temper, contented and cheerful, a perfect pattern of industry, chipping out holes in her log of wood, and flitting about with a happy little chirp from morning till night, a bright example of what a cheery life may be lived, even by a caged bird, when kindly treated and cared for thoughtfully.

TITMICE.

I MUST own my strong liking for these active, saucy little birds. For eighteen years I have always had a basket hung just outside the dining-room window containing their favourite food, *i.e.*, fat of any kind, cooked or uncooked; and most amusing it is to watch their little odd ways and tempers whilst frequenting the said basket. Four species thus studied showed distinct characteristics. Directly I put out a fresh supply of fat, the Cole Tit would spend all his time and energies in carrying it away, piece by piece, to lay by in store for the future, in crevices in the bark of trees, and this work he would carry on with misplaced energy until the basket was emptied. The Greater Tit and Marsh Tit came quietly for the supply of their own personal needs, and to feed their young in nesting time, but the Blue Tit was by far the most amusing. His attitudes were quite a study; he seemed rather to prefer being upside down; clinging to the basket and hammering away at the hard fat, head downwards, was a favourite pose; then, when any one else desired a share, he would make a stand with open beak and outspread wings and enact "king of the castle" in the most impertinent manner, considering his tiny dimensions. A guerilla warfare seems always going on amongst these Blue Tits. If one was in the basket and remaining perfectly still, I knew two or three others were meditating a sudden combined assault, but it seemed as if the steady gaze of the titmouse in possession kept them at bay for a time. At length a twittering scrimmage ensued, and the combatants disappeared. I once coaxed a Blue Tit to live in the dining-room for a few days, and he made himself very happy, constantly flitting about in search of insects, running up and down the curtains like a veritable mouse, alighting on any joint of cold meat which happened to be on the sideboard, and making an excellent dinner in Bohemian fashion. Of course his fearless curiosity led him into difficulties. He would sit on the edge of a jug and peer down to see what it might contain, and his plumage was not improved by the baths of milk or cocoa which he met with in the pursuit of knowledge of this kind. Some years ago an empty cocoa-husk with a hole at one end, furnished with nesting materials, was hung up just above the basket of fat. A large tit began to build in it, but unhappily for him a Blue Tit had also been house-hunting, and determined to settle in it. I saw the matter decided by a pitched battle between the two; they fought desperately, rolling over and over on the lawn, pecking, chirping, beating each other with their wings, like little feathered furies as they were.

At last it was ended, and Blue Tit was victor, It was pretty to see the tiny pair building their nest, with little happy twitterings and

TITMICE.

confabulations over each piece of moss or dried leaf, and so fearless were they that a large blind was often let down close to and over the husk without disturbing the inmates. When the hen bird was sitting, the cock would bring a green caterpillar for her every four or five minutes, and sometimes take her place on the nest. I often took the husk down from its nail to show the brave little bird sitting on her eggs. If touched she would hiss and set up her feathers, but did not leave her nest. When the young birds were hatched, the parents were incessantly at work from early morning till late at night bringing small caterpillars about every two minutes to supply the wants of the tiny brood. One can judge of the usefulness of these birds in ridding our gardens of insect pests by the amount consumed by this one pair. By a moderate calculation, and judging by what I saw one afternoon, I believe they must have brought 3,570 in the course of one week. At last the day came when five little blue heads peeped out of the entrance to the husk. One after another the little ones flew into branches near by; the last one I held in my hand for a while that I might draw its portrait. Fearing it might be hungry if I kept it too long, I placed it in a cage on the lawn, where the old birds found it and fed it for me through the bars. I then brought it in again, and having finished its likeness, had the pleasure of restoring it to its parents. The Blue and Cole Tit often choose the inside of a disused pump as their nesting-place. A Cole Tit built in an old pump in our grounds for many years, the curved spout being its mode of ingress and egress. I could open a small door and look at the pretty little hen on her nest, and then at her numerous family, and watch their growth till old enough to fly. Certainly young birds show a grand lesson of obedience, for creeping out into the world through a dark, curved pipe, must have seemed a rather perilous mode of exit. Another less fortunate Cole Tit built in a post-box placed by a garden gate, and seemed in no way disconcerted when letters came in suddenly around and upon her. She usually laid eighteen eggs in a deep, soft nest of moss and hair. As boys were apt to take this nest year after year, a lock was placed to the box to protect the little bird; but the genus boy has no pity, and through the slit for the letters, some cruel urchin, vexed at not being able to take the nest, put in a stick and killed the poor little mother and broke the eggs. For several years a Blue Tit chose to build her nest in the lower part of a stone vase in the garden. There was a hole for drainage in the bottom, and through this hole the little bird found a circular space just suited for her nest. That particular vase could not be filled with plants till long after all the rest were gay with flowers. We were obliged to wait till the domestic affairs of the Tit family were ended, else their fate would have been sad indeed. There is no doubt that these birds do contrive to secure their share of peas and other things in the kitchen garden, and are by no means favourites with the gardeners, but I still maintain that the good they do in destroying insects counterbalances their evil doings in other respects. However, they sometimes commit other misdemeanours. My head gardener came to me one day looking very serious, and began by asking what he was to do about "those Blue Tits." "Why, what have they been doing?" I asked. "Two of them have been sitting at the entrance of one of the hives, and they have picked off and killed every bee as it came out, and now they have begun upon a second hive." "Well, you had better hang up some potatoes stuck over with feathers, and that will frighten them away." "I've done that, ma'am, and they sit on the potatoes and look at me!" It was a trying case of utter contumacy, and at last I was obliged, for the sake of saving my bees, to let one little victim be shot and hung up as "an awful example" to the rest, and it proved an effectual remedy. My basket of fat used to prove very attractive all through the cold weather, when, I suppose, these tiny birds need the caloric it supplies; they always left off coming as soon as the days were warm and insects plentiful.

BLANCHE, THE PIGEON.

PIGEONS possess a great deal more individuality of character than any one would suppose who has only seen them in flocks picking up grain in a farmyard, like domestic fowls.

They show to better advantage when only a few pairs are kept and fed daily at some settled place; but to make really interesting pets two are quite sufficient, and may be made very amusing companions. Some species may possess more mental capacity than others. Those I have to speak of were snow-white trumpeters. A pair was sent to me, but, to my sorrow, I found on opening the basket that the male bird had escaped on the way; so I could only put the solitary hen in a cage, and do all that was possible in the way of plentiful food and kind care to make her happy; but all to no purpose. The poor bird pined and grew weaker every day, till she became unable to get up to her perch. I used, therefore, to go to her every evening and place her comfortably for the night; and she soon grew tame enough to like being caressed and talked to.

When spring returned I obtained a male pigeon, and hoped Blanche would accept him for a mate, but she showed a great deal of temper, and made him so unhappy that he had to be exchanged for another a fine snow-white bird like herself, and, happily, of such a forbearing disposition as to endure being considerably "hen-pecked." Now began the curious part of Blanche's history. The pair built a nest in a small pigeon-house close to my window, so that I was able to watch all the family arrangements with much interest Blanche liked to be with me for some hours in the morning, sitting on the table pluming herself, quite at ease, and when that operation was ended she generally seated herself on a large Bible which lay at one end of the dining-table, and there she usually went to sleep; a white dove resting on the Word suggested to one's mind many a beautiful emblematic thought. These visits to me were paid most regularly when a nest was finished and the eggs were being hatched; she then shared the duties of incubation by turns with her mate. He would sit patiently for four hours on the nest, while Blanche spent that time with me; then, punctually at the right moment, she would wake up, and, lazily stretching her wings, would fly out at the open window to see how affairs were getting on at home, and take her place on the nest for her appointed four hours.

She was a most eccentric bird in the matter of laying eggs. I sometimes found she had made me a present of one, neatly placed amongst my working materials! In fact, wherever she happened to be upon the table would be deemed by her a suitable place for laying; and, as I always conveyed the eggs to her nest, her little freaks did not much matter. But at last she took it into her wilful little head to lay her eggs in the coal-scoop, an arrangement which by no means improved her snowy plumage. She had a pretty crest, which curved over her head, and her feet were clothed with rather long feathers reaching to the claws. At our breakfast-time she would often sit close to my plate, letting me stroke her and draw out her pretty wings. I must own she was as conceited as any peacock, throwing herself on her side and stretching out a feathered foot, little dreaming how she was being laughed at for her affected attitudes. If she had a fault, it was her temper! I have seen her go up to her mate and give him a most uncalled-for peck, and he amiable bird! would bear all her unkindness so meekly, only answering by a propitiatory coo. Blanche reared many sons and daughters, but none were so interesting as herself. I ascribe her unusual tameness to the loving care bestowed upon her in her long illness. When once a bird's affections are won in that way they generally remain firm friends for life.

GERBILLES.

THESE curious little animals were brought to my notice by a scientific friend who had seen them at the Zoological Gardens, and heard that they were to be obtained there by applying to Mr. Bartlett.

As I always regretted the untimely death of my pet jerboa, I thought these little rodents would fill his place, and prove amusing pets. And, accordingly, I paid a visit to the Zoo, and found a whole colony of gerbilles of all ages living very amicably together in a large, strongly-built wooden box, with bran, oats, and nuts for provender.

It was no easy matter to secure a pair of suitable size and age. I could but admire the patience of the attendant who made persevering attempts to catch the nimble creatures for me, but they leaped and sprang about, darted through his fingers, disappeared into holes, and seemed to enjoy his discomfiture. At length a lively pair, with sleek skins and perfect tails, were securely caged.

Then I was warned to keep them in a tin-lined cage, as they would "gnaw through anything," even the solid teak chest in which they were kept was being rapidly demolished by their powerful incisors.

The gerbilles were placed in a plant case, four feet long, with glass sides and top, through which their gambols could easily be seen. The case had a glass partition, and on one side lived a pair of chipmunks, or striped American squirrels. They were highly incensed at their new neighbours, springing with all their force against the partition, with low growlings, casting up the cocoa fibre with their hind legs, as if to try and hide them from their view. They soon found a little chink, through which, I am afraid, some very strong language was launched at the new-comers.

Happily the gerbilles did not mind. They found delightful tree-roots to gnaw at, plenty of food, and freedom to frisk and frolic to their heart's content, so their neighbours were free to growl as much as they liked, and they in their turn raised a hill of fibre and played at hide-and-seek in their new domain.

But let me now describe these gerbilles. I believe there are several species, differing somewhat in appearance. These were fawn-coloured, with sleek, soft fur, which, like the chinchilla, was blueish next to the skin. They were about the size of small rats, with little ears and long tails, with a black tuft at the end. The fur was white underneath, the eyes jet black and very large, and long black whiskers, which were always in motion. The hind legs being longer than the front ones, enabled the creature to spring and leap along the ground with great rapidity, as I found to my cost one night, when five of them got out of their case and gave us an hour's occupation before they could be recaptured. One managed to get inside an American organ, and effectually baffled all our efforts to secure him. There was no help for it, he had to be left there, and I went away with an anxious mind as to what his busy teeth would be employed upon all night; and, sure enough, next morning a velvet curtain was found nibbled and tattered, and being converted into a nest for the enterprising gerbille! They became very amusing, tame little creatures, ready to take dandelions, nuts, or any little dainty, from one's hand.

As they breed very readily in England, I was soon presented with a little family of five very tiny, pinkish-coloured infants, quite blind, and destitute of hair. They were not attractive, and so were left to their mother's care till they could see and were properly clothed, and then they were extremely pretty, and rapidly developed all the habits and manners of their parents, gnawing wood, nibbling nuts, and having merry games of their own, darting with wonderful quickness in and out of the tree-roots, and getting up small battles for some coveted morsel of diet. The first pair were quiet enough, and agreed happily together, but when, later on, mother and daughter happened to have a little brood at the same time, things became complicated, and it was no uncommon sight to see the two mothers careering about, each with an infant in its mouth, and it often fell to my lot to take care of the unfortunate children and replace them in the nest whilst the mothers had a "stand-up" fight, and this is a literally true expression, for gerbilles sit bolt upright and fight each other with their front feet; but, though they appear to be in desperate conflict, I must say I never saw that any damage was done. As to their gnawing power, it is almost beyond description. I gave them a strong wooden box as a nursery for the young gerbilles, but before long they had eaten out the back and sides, and a mere skeleton of a box remained. There was a piece of zinc, which formed a partition, but they ate a hole right through the zinc in no time, and when a wire cage, with a sliding door, was placed in the plant case, they soon learnt how to lift up the door and get out. We often watched the formation of the family nest, which was constructed of wool and hay nibbled very small, and carried by mouthfuls and woven together. It generally had two outlets for ingress and egress. There the entire family would sleep during the day amicably enough, but towards evening the nursery disputes would begin, and old animosities led to frequent battles and scrimmages, because somebody wanted some one else's pieces of wool for the precious infants. Still they were very tame, amusing little creatures, liking to be stroked and fed and rewarded by a run upon the breakfast-table, where they would examine every dish and plate in a delicate, inquiring way, not touching the contents – only trying to add to their small amount of knowledge of the outside world. Their food consisted of bran, oats, pea-nuts, wheat, fresh dandelion and clover-leaves, and on these they lived in perfect health and beauty.

As the colony increased, it was needful to make several homes for the gerbilles, and the original pair happened to be, for a time, in a cage upstairs on a landing. One of these found its way out of the cage, down the stairs, across the hall, and was discovered next morning in a room where the younger members of the family were kept. This would go to prove a keen scent, which, I suppose, guided the little animal to find its friends, and also confirms what travellers have written about gerbilles living in large colonies and always keeping together.

One evening I had to read some natural history papers at a Band of Mercy meeting in a neighbouring village, where the clergyman's wife took great interest in promoting kindness to animals, and as I proposed speaking about the gerbilles, I thought I would take some of them with me to show the children. Accordingly a mother and four little ones were put into a cage with some food and bedding for their comfort whilst being exhibited. I was concerned to see the extreme terror they seemed to feel at the unusual motion of the carriage, and in a few minutes one became convulsed and literally died of fright. I held the cage in my lap, and talked to the others to reassure them, fearing more casualties, but after a while they settled down, and we reached the schoolroom in due time. I was scarcely prepared for the tremendous sensation the gerbilles created. Remarks in broad Hertfordshire greeted their appearance, "Whoy, here's a lot of moise." "Noa, they ain't; they's rats!" "Will they boite?" and then such a cluster of children came round me they had to be called to order, and the cage was carried round that all might see the little foreigners, and through all the after-proceedings many pairs of eyes remained fixed upon the cage and its inmates. I fancy that evening will long be remembered by the children.

The great difficulty that attends the keeping of these little animals is their rapid rate of increase. It is true they can all be kept together, for, as I have said, though there are squabbles they do not result in any personal injury, and thus my colony was allowed to go on till there was no counting the number of generations that existed. I very much wished to reduce the numbers, and give some away, but could never tell which were the mothers of the small pink infants I was being presented with continually. I tried putting a little family of the babies into a cage in the plant case, hoping the mother who belonged to them would then appear and take care of them; but no, the entire colony trooped in and ran riot in the new place, and if a young gerbille was by chance left uncovered in the *mélee*, a twentieth cousin would take it up tenderly as if it was its own mother, and replace it in the nest a very emblem of brotherly kindness and charity. The colony had finally to be dispersed and given away in small detachments to different friends, and, strange to say, in no other case did the numbers increase, I imagine because the requisite conditions of space and quietness were not realized as in the pleasant home I was able to provide for them.

WATER SHREWS.

HEARING that the little patients in a London hospital had scarcely any toys, and that they especially desired a very large doll, I had one dressed for them, and various other interesting items, such as an album of pictures, bags of shells, a stamp snake, &c., were prepared; but a large box was needed in which to pack all these treasures; and one which had been for months in the wine-cellar was brought up for that purpose into the hall.

It was filled with straw, and as I was watching this being taken out I noticed some small black animals darting about in it.

"They must be young rats," I exclaimed, "and the rare kind, too the black rat, which has been almost entirely eradicated by the stronger brown species." A curious instance, by the way, of a foreign interloper driving out the native.

I immediately resolved to secure these animals, whatever they might prove to be, and, armed with leather gloves, and an empty glass globe to place my captures in, I began to search in the straw, and soon secured the supposed rats, but they proved to be a pair of water shrews jet black, lively little creatures, with sharply-pointed snouts and teeth, as I soon discovered to my cost. I had taken off my gloves and was watching the activity of the shrews, when suddenly they flew upon each other, biting and screaming with rage, and, thinking they would kill each other at that rate, I tried to separate them, but one turned and bit me pretty severely, and it was with some difficulty they were parted. One I put into a zinc fern case, and the other into a large empty aquarium, with shingle at the bottom, moss and wool for bedding, and a large pan of water for swimming and bathing.

They were rather larger than the common mouse, jet black above, and greyish-white beneath restless, active creatures, usually found near ponds and ditches; and how ever these two had found their way into a dry cellar, and lived in a box of straw will always remain a mystery. I learnt from books that they fed on worms and insects, and that diet was provided, though much to my distress, for it is a miserable thing to see any living creature tortured and devoured alive, even though it may be in obedience to natural instincts. Happily I soon found a substitute. I was showing one of the shrews to a fellow-student of natural history, and with a long feather soon attracted the little animal's attention; he always came out of his bed and sprang upon the feather like a little tiger, dragging it about and holding on with the grip of a bull-dog, so that cne could lift him off the ground and keep him swinging a minute in the air to see the pretty white fur underneath. My friend suggested that it probably fed on small birds and thought the feather was part of its daily fare.

I obtained a fowl's head from the larder, and then it was a sight to see how it was pounced upon and dragged about until securely hidden under the moss, when we could hear our little friend crunching the bones and tearing it to pieces as if he had not had anything so good for a long while.

One shrew died in a few days, but the other lived three weeks in perfect health, and I believe it was an accidental failure of sufficient food that led to the death of the second; their appetite seems to be, like that of the mole, most voracious, and unless they obtain a constant and ample supply of food they quickly die of hunger.

They are worth studying for a few days, but their dreadful odour and fierce character make them anything but pets. I suppose there is hardly any animal in England so fierce and combative, and probably that may account for the fact that one so often comes across a dead shrew lying on the path in summer.

When swimming, the shrew's furry coat perfectly resisted the entrance of moisture; it always came out absolutely dry. The said coat was most carefully kept in order; a daily brushing and cleansing went on, the little tongue was often at work licking off every little speck of dust; the toes were spread out and examined; the small amount of tail kept in order. I could but think how many a lesson we may learn from the small as well as the great creations of God's hand habits such as this little animal possessed might, in the way of cleanliness, lead to the prevention of endless diseases, if imitated by those who never dream of daily cleansings as being necessary to health and life.

SQUIRRELS.

IF one lives in the country where these graceful little animals exist, it is well worth while to attract them near the house so that one may enjoy the sight of their gambols and minister to their wants by suitable diet As I have already said, for many years food was placed in a basket outside the dining-room window to attract the charming little titmice, and four species might be seen feasting on fat of different kinds. I placed Barcelona nuts for the nuthatches, and they came and shared the contents of the basket with the tits. The nuts also drew a squirrel to the spot, and after about a year, the little fellow became so used to seeing us moving in the room that he would sit in the basket with his graceful little tail curved over his back, cracking his nuts, and nibbling away quite at ease. Then the window was opened and the nuts put on a table inside the room, and there little "Frolic" sits whilst we are at meals and forms one of the family, holding his nuts cleverly in his paws, whilst his sharp teeth bite a hole in them, and, regardless of tidiness, he flings the shells about as he nibbles at the kernels, looking at us with his black, beady eyes, perhaps speculating upon what our breakfast may be. How much more enjoyable is this sort of pet than a poor caged squirrel whirling round in his wheel, condemned to a dreary life, with no freedom or change, no intercourse with his kind.

In town there is, perhaps, no way to keep a squirrel but in a cage; even so, by an occasional release from its captivity, a constant variety in its food, and its being talked to and noticed, its life may be made less irksome, and, if young, it may eventually be made quite tame, and become an interesting daily companion.

We derived great amusement from our squirrel visitors; one after another they would leap up the side of the window and spring in and out of the basket in quick succession, carrying away a nut at each visit, playing and skirmishing with each other in lively fashion. I am sorry to confess there was great jealousy amongst them. A second squirrel took to coming into the room, and Frolic and he had a pitched battle, in which our favourite, poor little fellow! lost half his ear, and a sponge and water were needed to efface the sanguinary stains left by the fight

The squirrel's great enemy is the cat. One would not think she could catch the agile little creature; but one day we saw a cat watching an unconscious little squirrel under the tulip-tree: we did not dream that she could harm it, but in a moment she made one swift rush at her prey. The squirrel ran at full speed, but alas! before we could interfere it was caught and carried away.

At Dropmore, the gardener told us he had a cat that kept the Pinetum quite clear of squirrels. They certainly nibble the young shoots of firs and horse-chestnuts unmercifully in the spring, and one very dry summer they took very kindly to our peaches and nectarines; but I freely forgive their little sins, and should be sorry to miss them from the lawn where there are often four or five to be seen at once.

They chase each other round a tree-stem with wonderful agility, and express their animosity with angry grunts and a stamp of the foot like a rabbit. In autumn I have acorns and beech-mast collected, and store some bushels of each to be doled out through the winter and spring; strewn under the tulip-tree this food, mixed with corn, attracts an amusing variety of live creatures. Besides the squirrels which are constantly there, we see jays, wood-pigeons, jackdaws, rooks, and flocks of the smaller birds; if snow should prevail, a whole rookery will come to see what is to be had. By constantly watching their movements I have learnt that the squirrel's tail has quite a language of its own. It can be curved over its back and so spread out that on a wet day it forms a complete shelter from rain. It will take the form of a note of interrogation or lie flat on the ground, stand out at an angle or bristle with anger, according to the mood of the possessor.

I did not find the American chipmunks, before alluded to, at all tameable. They were very handsome, of grey colour with dark brown stripes on their sides.

They were extremely wild, and would spring round their cage in perfect terror when looked at, so, finding they could not be made happy in confinement, I let them loose in the garden in the hope they might burrow under a large rhododendron clump, but after a day or two they disappeared, and I suppose they made their escape to a neighbouring wood, so that I have little hope of ever seeing them again.

A MOLE.

A LIVE mole above-ground is a somewhat rare sight, for, as a rule, his habits are altogether subterranean; but now and then he may be captured by a sudden grasp as he scrambles along in his odd, unwieldly fashion, and a curious fellow he is in many ways.

Strolling quietly along a country lane one summer's evening, I heard a great rustling in a dry ditch, the dead leaves were being scattered right and left, and I stopped to see what could be the cause. In a minute the black velvet coat of a mole appeared, and I at once resolved to endeavour to catch it, though with little hope of success, for the creature is apt to dive into the ground in an instant when alarmed. However, watching my opportunity, I managed to seize and hold him firmly; but I had nothing to put him in, and he struggled furiously to escape. All I could do was to roll him up in one end of my black lace shawl and hurry home with my capture. Alas! for the unlucky shawl the mole soon began rending and tearing it into shreds with his powerful feet and teeth. I was rapidly becoming acquainted with the habits of moles, and in a way that I should not soon forget; still, that mole must be brought home somehow, and I next transferred him to my dress pocket, which I held fast, whilst he scrambled and pushed his strong little snout in all directions to find some way of escape. He was soon placed in a zinc fern case, with glass sides, supplied with earth to burrow in, and fed with worms. I also gave him a pan of water, as I remembered seeing a plan of a mole's burrow which always includes a place for water. It was a really painful sight to watch the creature feeding; he pounced upon a worm with the fury of a tiger, and holding it in his mouth, tore it to pieces with his sharp claws and rapidly devoured all the pieces, and snuffing about to make sure he had quite finished it, he then darted off to seek another. The mole has a most voracious appetite and dies very quickly if unable to obtain food. I was interested to watch the bustling, active life of the little creature; his morning toilet when the black velvet coat was attended to, carefully brushed and licked by a tiny red tongue (though it never seemed to pick up dirt or defilement in its passage through the earth) and finally, after a few days, I had the pleasure of setting him free, when he dived into the ground out of sight in a moment.

Some years later a live mole was much desired by a young relative who was giving Natural History lectures to some school children. It happened that a mole had found its way into the conservatory and was doing much damage there by making its runs close to the surface and uprooting the plants in its course. The gardener and I resolved to catch it; he was anxious to prevent further mischief to his plants, and I was wishing to help the lecturer by sending a lively specimen to illustrate his subject. The exciting part of the business was the necessity of making the capture before eleven o'clock, when the carrier would pass by, and, taking charge of the animal, would deliver it in time for the lecture next day. We watched for the upheaving of the mole's run which came at last The gardener made a quick plunge with his hand into the soft earth, but alas! the mole escaped. He kept quiet for ten minutes, then another attempt was made, and failed. The carrier's bell sounded and he passed by. I still kept watch, and again saw the earth move the third time was successful. I had gone to find a tin box, and on my return I was greeted with "Here's the mole, ma'am!" Poor fellow! he was being ignominiously held up by the scruff of his neck, and kicking furiously at the indignity. He was soon packed up in soft grass, with a plentiful supply of worms to feast upon by the way. A special messenger overtook the carrier, and a telegram was sent to announce the dispatch of the precious animal.

He first reached a London office, where I fear he tended to hinder business, as it was needful to transfer him to a cage, and no one seemed particularly anxious for the honour of catching him, as his teeth were known to be both sharp and numerous, and his disposition not of the meekest However, he was placed in his cage, travelled down into Kent, and gave wonderful pleasure when exhibited to the children.

One would naturally suppose that in a country village where boys and girls are daily going to and from school, they would all have been familiar with this little creature, but when the question was asked if they had ever seen a dead mole, only fifteen children out of ninety had seen one, and only three had ever seen a live one.

Next day the mole was let loose upon a very hard piece of ground, but even there he very quickly burrowed out of sight.

HARVEST MICE.

I HAD often wished to keep these interesting little animals, but as they are only found in some parts of England and are difficult to capture from their minute size and delicacy, I had to wait many years before they could be obtained. At length, through the kindness of a friend, six were sent to me from Norfolk, and for two years they lived in captivity and afforded me much pleasure.

They are the smallest English rodents, two of them only weighing a halfpenny; they are brown in colour with white underneath, very long whiskers and prehensile tails. They were made happy by finding all things needful for their comfort in a large plant case. A thick layer of cocoa fibre was spread over the bottom of the case, dry moss and hay provided, wheat-ears, oats, and canary seed, and a small cup of water. A flowerpot in which a number of small branches were fixed afforded opportunity for exercise in climbing, and a pleasant resting-place was formed by a half-cocoanut filled with cotton-wool and roofed over with dry moss, then slung by three wires in a tripod of sticks of corky-barked elm, a little hole for entrance being left at one side. Into this the mice went the moment they were turned into the case, and in it they mostly lived. I fancy its swinging a little as they moved inside was congenial to their ideas of comfort. As they live in cornfields and make a pendulous nest attached to an ear of corn, I supplied them with a pot of growing wheat, in the hope that they would incline to make a nest in it; but I could never induce them to rear a family. They would sit for hours in the corn-stalks and nibble them into a heap of shreds, but no nest ever appeared. Their greatest delight was a handful of fresh moss full of little insects on which they would feed. The greatest excitement was always shown when the moss appeared little heads would peep out of the cocoa-husk, little noses sniffed in all directions, and then, with jerky runs, the tiny folk made their way to the attractive spot, and soon each would be seen sitting up like a small kangaroo feasting on a beetle or spider held in the tiny paws. Sometimes in their great happiness they made a low, sweet chirping like a company of wrens conversing cheerily together. When climbing in their tree-branches it was interesting to see how the fine wiry tail was always coiled round the stem as the creature descended, so as to keep it from falling and injuring itself.

Canary seed and brown bread seemed a favourite diet, and if I put a trough of growing corn into the case the mice made little burrow? through it so as to be able to eat the wheat from below. I had heard a sad report that my fairy-like pets had a tendency to eat each other as spring came round! This I fancied might arise from lack of animal food, so once or twice a week I always gave them a small portion of meat and this seemed to prevent any tendency to cannibalism.

After keeping them two years several deaths occurred, so I thought the remainder should have their liberty, and I had the pleasure of seeing them enter one of my corn-stacks where I hope they found all that their little hearts could desire, and possibly they would stray to a neighbouring bank and found a colony.

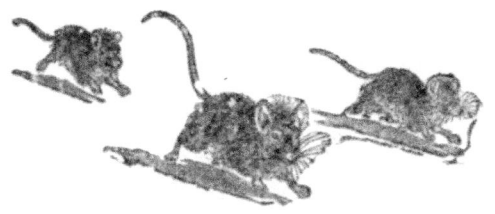

THE CALIFORNIA MOUSE.

A RATHER strange parcel from California reached me by post some years ago. It was marked "Live animals with care," and consisted of a box, containing several divisions, each having fine wire-work to admit air. In one I found a spiny creature called a Gecko, in another a beautiful lizard which had not survived the journey, and in the third a very rare species of mouse known as *Perognathus Pencillatus*. It has a soft silky coat of silver grey and fawn colour, and a long tail with a little tuft at the end, very large black eyes and white paws. It was alive, but weak and tired with its journey of ten days and all the jars and shocks it must have had by the way. I gave it warm milk and soaked bread, which it seemed to enjoy, and some hours later it was supplied with wheat grains, the food upon which it lives in its native country.

True to his natural instinct, mousie soon began to fill both his cheek pouches with the corn, and tried to hide it away as a supply for the future. In a few days the little creature was in perfect health, and he has been a great pet now for several years; perfectly tame and gentle, he will run about on the table and amuse himself happily wherever he is placed.

Being entirely inodorous he is kept in the drawing-room in a mahogany cage which was made specially to meet his small requirements. He is a busy little creature at night, as he likes daily to make a fresh bed of cotton-wool, and fusses about with his mouth full of material until he has arranged his little couch.

In his own country, where the cold is very severe in winter, its habit is to become perfectly unconscious, exactly as if dead, and in that state it can endure the rigour of the climate and wake up when the temperature rises. It was once left in a cold room and became in this apparently lifeless state. I was not alarmed, as I knew of its peculiarity, but it really was difficult to believe it ever could revive; there was no trace of warmth, or any apparent beating of the heart, and so it lay for some days, but on bringing it into a warm room it became as bright and active as ever. It seems a more intense form of hibernation than that of our squirrel and dormouse.

The naturalist at San Bernardino, from whom I obtained this mouse, told me he had kept one as a pet for many years, and his specimen lived entirely without water, as there was sufficient moisture in the wheat grains on which it fed to supply its need; but I think it is cruel to keep anything without the means of quenching thirst which might arise from an artificial mode of life, so my little pet has always a small jar of water to which I know it resorts from its requiring to be refilled from time to time.

SANCHO THE TOAD.

ABOUT four years ago I began to feed a toad that had found its way into the conservatory. He sat daily in one place expecting his meal-worms, and when he had snapped them up with his curious sticky tongue he would retire to some hidden nook and be invisible until the next day. Each winter he has hibernated as soon as cold weather began, and reappeared with the spring sunshine. Sancho is now a very portly, and most amusing pet.

Few people would guess how much character can be shown by even this poor, despised reptile when treated with real kindness, regularly fed, and never frightened or abused. I will describe what happens when Sancho is "shown to the public."

Some meal-worms are thrown on the pavement near him. He sits for a time gazing at them with his gold-rimmed eyes; then slowly creeps towards them, fixes his eyes on one of the worms bends his head a little towards it, then one hears a snap and the prey is taken. The act is so rapid that one can never see the tongue that has picked up the meal-worm simply it is gone! The toad's eyes are tightly shut whilst he swallows the morsel, and then he turns to pick up a second. Now is the time to approach him from behind and begin to stroke his leathery, warty skin. In a few seconds he is in a state of perfect ecstasy, his front legs are stretched out, he leans first to one side, then to the other, to guide the hand where he wishes to be stroked, and at last uplifts his ponderous body until he is an inch or more from the ground, supported on the tips of his toes. No description can do justice to the absurdity of the attitude, and the rapture seems so intense that food is forgotten, and so long as Sancho can get any one to stroke him, he is quite oblivious to all around him, although at other times he will hop away as soon as any stranger approaches.

Sancho will not, as yet, take anything from my hand, but I hope to bring him to that state of tameness in course of time.

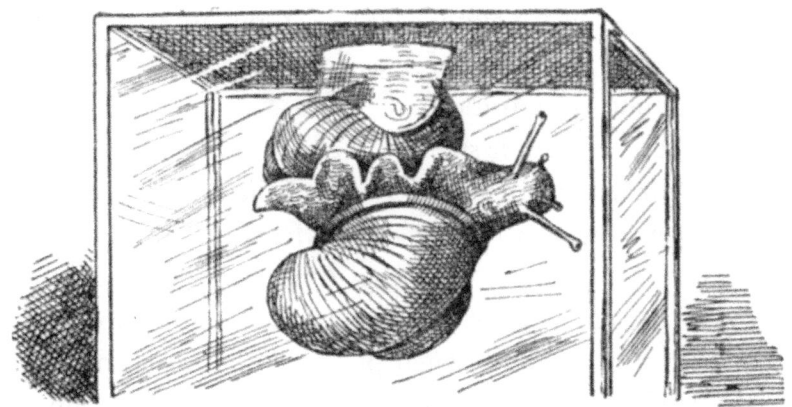

ROMAN SNAILS.

ROMAN SNAILS.

"HOW *can* you take an interest in snails and slugs?—horrid, slimy, crawling things!" More than once have I heard this kind of remark from youthful lips when I produced my grand old Roman snails and gave them a pleasant time for exercise upon the dewy lawn. Now in my secret mind I think a snail is a wonderfully curious creature, neither ugly nor "horrid"—it is slimy, but about that I shall have something to say later on.

When staying at Box Hill, near Dorking, I often saw the great apple snail, *Helix Pomatia*, which is only found on chalk soils, and is supposed to have been introduced by the Romans, from the quantities of their empty shells found with Roman remains in all parts of England. They were kept and fattened in places called "Cochlearia" and made into various "dainty dishes" which the Romans thought quite fit to set before their kings. It is certain that they are very nutritious creatures, and that in times of famine people have supported life and kept themselves mysteriously "fat and well-liking" by resorting to snails and slugs as articles of diet. Indeed I have heard more than once that the famous "Pâte de Guimauve" owes its healing nutritive character to this despised univalve, which is said to enter largely into its composition.

I brought several apple snails home with me from Box Hill and kept them for many years, until I really believe the creatures, in a dim sort of way, recognized me as their friend, or at any rate their feeder. I cannot boast, as I believe an American lady is said to have done, that "her tame oysters followed her up and down stairs," but certainly my snails would, when placed upon the lawn, very frequently crawl towards me, and would do so again and again when removed to a distance. As the weather became cold they always hibernated, closing the mouth of the shell with a thin, firm covering, or operculum, of chalk, which, mixed with their slime, made a substance like plaster of Paris. Thus enclosed they would lie as if dead until the warmth of the following spring made them push the door open and come out, with excellent appetites, ready to eat voraciously to make up for their long fast. These Roman snails were quite five inches long when fully extended, and therefore were much larger than our English species; the body was cream colour and the shell a pale tint of buff varying somewhat in different specimens.

These creatures were kept in a fern case with glass top and sides, and it was singular to observe the way in which they could suspend themselves (as shown in the drawing) from the top of the box.

The substance which exists in the caterpillar of the silkworm moth, and which can be drawn out into fine shreds of silk, is very similar to the slime of the snail, only in the latter it is not filiform, but exudes as a liquid and then hardens into a thin layer of silk which is strong enough to support the weight of two of these snails, for, seeing them one day thus suspended, I put them in the scales and ascertained that the weight of the two amounted to 2½ ounces.

This mucus forms the glistening, shiny track which the snail leaves behind it, enabling it to glide easily and painlessly over rough substances which would otherwise lacerate its soft body.

One hardly expected to find social feeling and affection in animals so low down in the scale of nature, but I do not know what else could have led my "Romans" to caress each other with their long horns by the hour together and always keep close to one another, twisting and curling their yielding bodies round each other in the most odd contortions. Our English snails hibernate in whole colonies for the winter, which also points to their affectionate and gregarious habits.

In lifting up some moss I once came upon some yellow, half-transparent eggs about as large as pearl barley, and wishing to know what they would prove to be I kept them in damp moss under a tumbler for about a fortnight, when, to my dismay, I found a grand colony of yellow slugs! and not a little was I teased about these interesting young people. I am afraid I must own they were given as a *bonne bouche* to my Virginian nightingale, who seemed highly to approve of this addition to his daily fare. Snails' eggs are nearly white and semi-transparent; the empty shells of young snails are very lovely when placed in a good microscope: the polariscope bringing out their exquisite prismatic tints.

The gardener one day brought in a testacella, or shelled slug. It fed upon earth-worms and was quite unlike the ordinary black or grey slug, of which we have, alas! countless thousands preying upon all the green things of the earth. This shelled slug was yellow, and seemed able to elongate its body very differently to any other species. The shell was quite small, a simple dome-shaped plate upon the anterior part of the body. I kept it for some weeks on damp moss under a tumbler but it was often able to escape by flattening itself to a mere thread and then crawling under the rim of the tumbler, and at last I gave it liberty as a reward for its persevering efforts to obtain its freedom.

AN EARWIG MOTHER.

HAD often read of the earwig as an incubating insect, and much wished to see for myself how she carried out her motherly instincts. One bright May morning found me busily turning over stones, clinkers, and old tree-roots in a fernery, which, having been long undisturbed, seemed a likely spot for the nest I wished to find. There seemed no scarcity of worms, wood-lice, centipedes, or beetles, but no earwigs could I see; and I was just about to give up the search when, lifting a piece of stone, I saw a small cavity, about as large as would contain a pea, and in it lay about twenty-six round, white eggs, hard-shelled and shining, of the size of a small pin's head. An earwig had placed herself over the eggs, and I was delighted to think at last I had lighted upon the insect mother I had been searching for. But what was to be done with her? How could I watch the process of incubation? The difficulty was solved by lifting the nest and its mother with a trowel and placing it in a saucer under a tumbler, without any displacement of the eggs; thus the mother's care could be conveniently watched. The earwig first carefully examined her new home, touching each morsel of earth and stone with her antennae; and, having ascertained the exact condition of things, she set to work to make a fresh nest, labouring with great industry until it was formed to her mind. She then took up the eggs, one by one, with her mandibles, and placed them in the new nest, arranging and rearranging them, until at last she seemed content, and remained either upon or near them for the rest of the day, quite motionless.

Every night, and sometimes two or three times in the day, she would form fresh places in the earth, and replace the eggs. To prevent the soil becoming too dry, I used to sprinkle a little water upon it a drop here and there and if by accident the water fell too near the eggs, the earwig became much excited, hurrying to and fro with her eggs, until they were all removed to a drier spot On the other hand, if I omitted the water until the earth became dry, she would choose the dampest spot that remained in which to form her nest, and seemed to welcome the water-drops, drinking herself from them, and feeling the damp earth with her antennae. She remained thus for three weeks, feeding on little pieces of beef or mutton, or an occasional fly; I did not then know that earwigs are mostly vegetable feeders, but it is clear they can eat other food when needful. The first time I dropped a newly-killed house-fly near her she looked at it intently, felt it with her antennae, and then suddenly wheeled round and pinched it with her forceps, and being apparently satisfied that it could do no harm to her eggs, she began to devour it, and after an hour or two but little remained except the wings.

As it was early in the year, but few insects could be seen, but by searching in the conservatory I found a large green aphis, which I gave to the earwig. To my surprise, instead of devouring it at once, she applied herself to one of the projecting tubes of the aphis, and evidently sucked its sweet secretion, and enjoyed it as much and in the same way as ants are said to do. She feasted thus for four or five minutes, but I am sorry to add that, unlike the humane ants, who care tenderly for their aphides and preserve their lives by kind treatment, the earwig ended by munching up the unfortunate aphis, till not a trace of it was left.

At the end of three weeks I found one morning all the eggs were hatched, and tiny, snow-white earwigs, with forceps and antennae fully developed, were creeping about and around their mother. I placed a slice of pear in the saucer, upon which the little ones swarmed, and seemed to find it congenial food. In a few days they increased to nearly double their size when first hatched, and turned a light brown colour. Having ascertained all I wished to know about the maternal instincts of the earwig, I released the mother and her family, and no doubt she was happy enough to return to her old haunt in the fernery, and would greatly prefer tree-roots and stones to my tumbler-and-saucer arrangement

THE SACRED BEETLE.

IN reading books on Egypt and the voyage up the Nile, one is sure to find some mention of the curious beetle which is found along the banks of the river, especially in Nubia, where the shore is traceried with the footprints of the busy little creature. Miss Edwards, in her very interesting book, "A Thousand Miles up the Nile," thus speaks of it: "Every one knows how this scarab was adopted by the Egyptians as an emblem of creative power and the immortality of the soul; it is to be seen in the wall-sculptures, on the tombs, cut out in precious stones and worn as an ornament, buried in the mummy-cases, and a figure of the beetle forms a hieroglyph, and represents a word signifying 'To be and to transform.' If actual worship was not paid to Scarabceus Sacer,* it was, at any rate, regarded with the greatest reverence and a vast amount of symbolism drawn from its various characteristics."

I had often wished to see this insect alive, and one day my wish was very unexpectedly gratified by the arrival of a small tin box in which I found a specimen of the sacred beetle swathed in wet linen like a veritable mummy, only, instead of being an Egyptian specimen, this had come from a kind friend at the Riviera, who knew

*Or *Ateuchus Sacer.*

that the same species existed there, and had sent me this one by post. The scarab was at once named "Cheops," and treated with all the respect due to his ancient family traditions.

His wants were easily supplied: a deep tin box, with earth and moss slightly damped, gave him space for exercise; and then for food alas! that his tastes should be so degraded he had to be supplied with cow-dung! This could be done in secret, and judiciously hidden by fair, green moss; but when exhibiting my cherished pet to admiring friends the first question was sure to be, "What does he feed upon?" and one had to take refuge in vague generalities about organic substances, &c., which might mean anything, and then, by diverting attention to some point of interest apart from the food question, the difficulty was generally overcome.

I kept a close watch to see if the beetle would be led by instinct to form its round pellets of mud as is its custom on the banks of the Nile, and having placed its egg in the centre, it begins to roll it from the margin of the river until it is above high-water mark. There it digs a hole and buries the pellet, leaving the sun to hatch the eggs in due time. Travellers who have watched the process describe the untiring way in which both the male and female beetle roll these pellets, often falling down with their burden into holes and ridges in the rough ground; but then their comrades will give them help, and, picking up the ball, they patiently labour on. Walking backwards, having the pellet between their broad hind legs, they push it up and up until it is placed in safety. The persevering energy of this insect led the Egyptians to adopt it as an emblem of the labours of their great deity, Osiris, or the sun; they also traced a resemblance in the spiny projections on its head to the rays of the sun.

Great was my delight to find at length that Cheops even in captivity was true to his native instincts, that he had formed a pellet about the size of a marble and was gravely rolling it with his hind legs backwards and forwards in his box. Poor captive! he was evidently puzzled what to do with the precious thing. He had no Nile bank to surmount, and the sun was hardly warm enough to encourage any hope for his future family; but he did the only thing that was possible he set to work to scoop out a hole of sufficient size, then rolled the pellet in and covered it over with loose earth. Three such pellets were made at intervals of a few days; one of them I unearthed and kept as a curio. The beetle never seemed to miss it, and having done his duty under difficult circumstances, his mind seemed to be at rest.

I often placed Cheops in my hand to show him to visitors, and there he would lie feigning to be dead until he was gently stroked over the elytra, when he would stretch out his antennae, then his legs by slow degrees appeared (for he tucked them close to his body out of sight when frightened), and at last he would begin to walk in a jerky manner, as if moved by machinery, often stopping to look and listen to be sure that it was safe to move, and even if busily at work in the earth, if he saw any one coming near he would stop, draw in his antennae and limbs and remain motionless.

He had a strong and peculiar odour at times, which became more apparent if he was annoyed. He was infested with a small mite, and though these were frequently cleared away with water and a camel's-hair brush, they always reappeared in a day or two, clustering under the thorax between the first pair of legs, and at times they might be seen racing over his body with great rapidity. Once Cheops nearly escaped, for I had placed his box in the sun, and the warmth so excited and waked him up that he opened his wing-cases, used his gauze-like inner wings, and with a mighty hum was all but gone in search of his native land, but fortunately I was near enough to intercept his flight and place him in safe quarters. After keeping this curious creature in perfect health for sixteen months, I was much vexed to find him one morning lying in a shallow pan of water in his box, quite dead. He had overbalanced on to his back, and, being unable to turn over, had been drowned, though the water was scarcely half an inch deep. Poor Cheops is enshrined in a pyramid-shaped box, in which he is often shown and his life-history told to interested visitors.

SPIDERS.

OF all the varieties of "creeping things" spiders seem to be the most universally disliked. I knew well the kind of expression I should see on the faces of my friends when I produced the box which contained my pet Tegenaria, a large black spider, long-legged and very swift, a well-known kind of house-spider.

Happily the box had a glass lid, so the inmate could be seen in comfort; and when the spider's history was told there was always an interest created in even this poor despised creature.

When first placed in its new home the Tegenaria began spinning tunnels of white silky web in various directions across the box. They were almost as close in texture as fine gauze, and had openings here and there, so that they formed a kind of labyrinth.

The spider always lived in one corner, curled up, watching for prey, and when a blue-bottle was put in, and began buzzing, she then rushed up one tunnel and down another until she could pounce upon her prey.

The fly was quickly killed by her poison fangs, and then carried to the corner to be consumed at leisure. Unlike the habit of the garden or diadem spider, no cobweb was rolled round the victim; only the wings were cut off and the body carried away. After some months I noticed the corner seemed filled up with web and fragments of insects, and when I examined it more closely there appeared a large round ball of eggs, over which the spider had spun some web, and then had collected all the legs and wings of her prey and stuck them carelessly here and there in the web so as to conceal her nest, and make it look like the remains of an old cobweb. Over this nest she kept careful watch. One could not drive her from it; she only left it for a moment to spring upon a fly, and would return with her food immediately and resume her watchful life in the corner. At length the young spiders were hatched in countless numbers; they crept about the tunnels, and though so minute as to be mere specks, they were perfect in form, active in seeking for prey, and appeared perfectly able to take care of themselves and begin life on their own account.

I had kept the Tegenaria more than a year in confinement, and having shown such admirable motherly instincts, I thought she had earned the reward of liberty. No doubt she welcomed "the order of release"! At any rate, she scampered away under some tree-roots, and possibly resides there with her numerous family to this day.

Spiders hunt their prey in a variety of ways—some by spinning their beautiful web, with which we are all familiar; others, as the Zebra spiders, catch flies by leaping suddenly upon them, and these may often be seen on window-sills watching some coveted insect, drawing slowly nearer to the victim, till, by a well-directed spring, it can be secured. There are nearly three hundred species of spiders in this country, and nearly all spin and weave their silken threads in some way, but each in different fashions, according to their mode of life. The female spider is the spinner, and her supply is about 150 yards. When she has used that amount a few days' rest will enable her to secrete a similar quantity.

With great pains the spider's silk has been obtained and woven into a delicate kind of material; but as each spider only yields one grain of silk, and 450 were required to produce one yard, the process was found to be impracticable. The insect possesses silk of two colours, silver-grey and yellow; one is used for the foundation-lines of the web, and the other for the interlacing threads. The silk is drawn by the spider from its four spinnerets, and issues from them in a soft, viscid state, but it hardens by exposure to the air. If a web is examined with a magnifying-glass, it will be seen that its threads are closely studded with minute globules of gum, which is so sticky that flies caught in the web are held in this kind of birdlime until the spider is able to spring upon them.

Astronomers and microscopists make use of the strongest lines of the spider's web to form some of their delicate instruments. The thread is drawn in parallel lines at right angles across the field of the eye-piece at equal distances, so as to make a multitude of fine divisions, scarcely visible to the naked eye, and so thin as to be no obstacle to the view of the object. One means of classifying spiders is by the number of eyes they possess. These are usually two, six, or eight in number. The fangs with which the spider seizes its prey are hollow, and emit a venomous fluid into the body of the victim, which speedily benumbs and kills it. In Palestine and other countries a kind of spider is found which is entirely nocturnal in its habits, and never either hunts or feeds in daylight, but makes itself a little home, where it abides safely till sunset. It is called the trap-door spider, from the curious way in which it protects the entrance to its nest. It bores a hole in the dry earth of a bank a foot or more in depth, lines the hole with silk, and forms a lid, or trap-door, which secures the spider from all intruders. I have one of these nests in which the door is a wonderful piece of mechanism, quite round and flat, about as large as a three-penny piece, made of layers of fine earth moistened and worked together with silk, so that it is tough and elastic and cannot crumble. The hinge is made of very tough silk, and is so springy that when opened it closes directly with a snap. The outside is disguised with bits of moss, glued on so that no one can see where the door is. The only way of opening it is with a pin, and even then the spider will hold on inside with his claws, so that it is not easy to overcome his resistance. Amongst some insects sent to me from Los Angelos is a huge "Mygale," a hairy monster of very uninviting aspect. When its legs are outspread it measures nearly six inches across, and one can well believe the stories one hears of its killing small birds if it finds them on their nests. A gentleman living in Bermuda is said to have tamed a spider of the species "Mygale," and made it live upon his bed-curtain and rid him of the flies and mosquitoes which disturbed his nightly rest. He thus describes this remarkable pet: "I fed him with flies for a few days, until he began to find himself in very comfortable quarters, and thought of spinning a nest and making his home. This he did by winding himself round and round, combing out the silk from the spinnerets at the end of his body till he had made a nest as large as a wine-glass, in which he sat motionless until he saw a fly get inside our gauzy tent; then I could fancy I saw his eyes twinkle as his victim buzzed about, till, when it was within a yard or so of him, he took one spring and the fly was in his forceps, and another leap took him back to his den, where he soon finished the savoury morsel. Sometimes he would bound from side to side of the bed and seize a mosquito at every spring, resting only a moment on the net to swallow it. In another corner of the room was the nest of a female Mygale of the same species. She spun some beautiful little silk bags, larger than a thimble, of tough yellow silk, in each of which she laid more than a dozen eggs. When these hatched the young spiders used to live on her back until they were old enough to hunt for themselves. I kept my useful friend on my bed for more than a year and a half, when, unfortunately, a new housemaid spied his pretty brown house, pulled it down, and crushed under her black feet my poor companion." This kind of spider, or an allied species, captures large butterflies in the tropical woods by hanging strong silken noozes from branches of trees, and they have been seen to kill small birds by this method. One of our British spiders lives under water in a dome-like cell of silk, which is filled with air like a diving-bell by the spider carrying down successive globules of air between its legs, which it liberates under the dome until it is filled; and the young are hatched there.

The spider, on its way through the water, never gets wet It is hairy, and is enveloped in a bubble of air, in which it moves about protected from wet and well supplied with air to breathe. As the spider's supply of food is always precarious, they are able to live a long time without eating. One is known to have lived eighteen months corked up in a phial, where it could obtain no food; but though thus able to fast, the spider is a voracious feeder, and will eat his own kith and kin when hard pressed by hunger.

I believe it is now thought that the spider of the Scriptures was a kind of spiny lizard called the Gecko. One of this species was sent to me from California, and lived for a few weeks, but as nothing would induce it to eat, to my great regret it pined and died. It was about as large as an ordinary full-grown toad, of a speckled grey colour, with rich brown markings, its head something like a lizard, with large thorny projections which extended all along the spine. The feet were very remarkable, each toe being furnished with a sucker which enabled the Gecko to walk with perfect ease in any position on a wall or pane of glass without losing its hold; and travellers say that it is a frequent inmate of Eastern houses, and may be seen catching flies as it creeps along walls and ceilings.

Many kinds of spiders run with ease upon the surface of ponds and ditches, and one forms a kind of raft of a few dead leaves woven together, on which it sits and is blown by the wind hither and thither, and thus is enabled to prey upon various aquatic insects.

The surface of grass lawns may be seen on autumnal mornings covered with tiny webs gemmed with dew. We may therefore estimate the immense number of flies captured by these traps so thickly spread over the grass, and see in them another proof of the adaptation of each created thing for its special purpose, and how wonderfully the balance of nature is maintained, so that one creature keeps another in check, and all work harmoniously together, according to the will of our great Creator

TAME BUTTERFLIES.

IN *The Century*, for June, 1883, Mr. Gosse I described a monument, in which the sculptor had carved a child holding out her hand for butterflies to perch on. He went on to say that this was criticised as improbable, even by so exact an observer as the late Lord Tennyson.

It may therefore be of some interest to record the following facts from my personal experience.

One summer I watched the larvae of the swallow-tailed butterfly through their different stages, and reserved two chrysalides to develop into the. perfect insect. In due time one of these fairy-like creatures came out I placed it in a small Indian cage, made of fine threads of bamboo. A carpet of soft moss and a vase of flowers in the centre made a pleasant home for my tiny "Psyche."

I found that she greatly enjoyed a repast of honey; when some was placed on a leaf within her reach, she would uncoil her long proboscis and draw up the sweet food with great apparent enjoyment

She was so tame that it became my habit, once or twice a day, to take her on my finger; and while I walked in the garden she would take short flights hither and thither, but was always content to mount upon my hand again. She would come on my finger of her own accord, and, if the day was bright, would remain there as long as I had patience to carry her, with her wings outspread, basking in the sunbeams which appeared to convey exquisite delight to the delicate little creature.

I never touched her beautiful wings. She never fluttered or showed any wish to escape, but lived three weeks of tranquil life in her tiny home; and then having, as I suppose, reached the limit of butterfly existence, she quietly ceased to live.

On the day of her death the other butterfly emerged, and lived for the same length of time. Both were equally tame, but the second showed more intelligence, for she discovered that by folding her wings together she could easily walk between the slender bars of the cage; and having done so she would fly to a window, and remain there basking in the sun, folding and unfolding her wings with evident enjoyment, until I presented my finger, when she would immediately step upon it and be carried back to her cage.

The tameness of these butterflies I ascribed in great measure to the fact of their having been hatched from chrysalides, and having therefore never known the sweets of liberty. I often wondered if really wild specimens could be won by gentle kindness and made happy in confinement, and one bright summer's day I resolved to try. A "Painted Lady" had been seen in the garden the day before, and I soon caught sight of her making rapid flights from one bed of flowers to another, and when resting for a few minutes, folding and unfolding her wings on the gravel path, I crept slowly up to her with a drop of honey on my finger to try and make friends; but my "lady" was coy, "she would and she wouldn't," and after letting me come within a few inches with my tempting repast, she floated away, out of sight, and I feared she would not be willing to give me another chance; however, I waited quietly, and in a few minutes she alighted at a little distance. I again drew near very slowly, and again she sailed away, but the third time she gained confidence enough to reach out her proboscis and taste the honey, and finally crept upon my finger. I very gently placed the light bamboo cage over her and brought her indoors; she, all the while, entranced with the sweet food, remained quietly on my finger, and when satisfied, crept upon a flower in the middle of the cage, and after a few flutterings round her cage seemed content and folded her delicate wings to rest. Whilst engaged in her capture I had observed a "Red Admiral" hovering over some dahlias, and thinking "Cynthia." might like a companion, I tried my blandishments upon him. The former Latin name for the "Painted Lady" butterfly I had not much hope of success, for though a bold, fearless fellow, he is very wary, and his powerful wings bear him away in swift flight when alarmed. Many a circle did I make around that dahlia bed! "Admiral" always preferred the opposite side to where I stood, and calmly crossed over whilst I went round. At last, by long and patient waiting, he, too, allowed me to come near and present my seductive food to his notice–the wiry proboscis was uncoiled and felt about for the honey; once plunged into that, all volition seemed to cease, he allowed me to coax him upon my finger, and he, too, was safely caged; but he behaved very differently from "fair Cynthia." The moment his repast was ended he flapped with desperate force against the bars, and in a minute he was out and on the window-pane, fluttering to escape. The cage had to be secured with fine net, and he was replaced and soon quieted down. Twice a day these delicate little pets would come upon my hand to receive their sweet food, and appeared perfectly content in captivity.

ANT-LIONS.

(Myrmeleon Formicarius.)

MANY years ago a friend sent me some of these remarkable insects from the Riviera, and for sixteen months I fed them as regularly as possible, but the cold of a remarkably severe winter killed them, to my great disappointment, as I had hoped to be rewarded by a sight of the perfect insect.

Ant-lions are not, I believe, found in any part of England, so I had to wait till I could again procure some from the south of France, where they are frequently met with in dry, sandy places.

Early in March this year (1890) three specimens were sent me and were at once placed in a box of dry silver sand, where they buried themselves and remained quietly resting for some hours.

Many of my readers may be interested to know what the ant-lion is like, and why I thought it worth while to take great pains to rear it. These young specimens were flat, grey, six-legged creatures about the size of a small lady-bird, covered with hairs, and possessing two strong forceps projecting from their heads. They are so formed that they cannot go forward, but move always backward by a series of jerks. As they live upon ants and are so strangely formed, they have to resort to stratagem in order to entrap their prey, and this they do by means of pits formed in the sand in which they live; into these pits the ants fall, and are seized by the forceps of the ant-lion, who lies in wait at the bottom.

Many a time have I watched the formation of these pits, and will try to describe the process. The insect begins describing a small circle on the surface of the sand by jerking himself backwards and flinging the sand away with his flat head and closed forceps, which form a kind of shovel. Each circle is smaller than the last, until the pit is like an inverted cone, and the ant-lion lies buried at the bottom, only his forceps being visible. When an ant has fallen headlong down into the pit it makes frantic efforts to escape, and if the ant-lion sees that it is likely to get beyond his reach, he then with his forceps flings some sand at it with such unerring aim the poor victim is sure to roll over and over until it reaches the jaws of its captor, who feasts upon it and then flings the remains of the body out of the pit

One difficulty was how to ensure a supply of ants, but this was overcome by filling a box with part of an ants' nest, and as these insects settled down and seemed content with their quarters, they were ready when wanted, and three times a day the lions had to be fed! One learns to sacrifice one's feelings in the cause of science, but to the last it was a real distress to me to have to put the poor little ants where they would be devoured; but Nature is cruel, and from the real lion to his insect namesake, preying upon one another seems the prevailing law of her realm.

As the ant-lions grew, the pits increased in size. At first they were about as large as a threepenny-piece, but ended by measuring more than two inches across.

I could not tell whether the insect moulted its skin, as it was always hidden, but in July, after four months' feeding, the ant-lions changed into chrysalides, which looked like perfectly round balls of sand.

The box was placed in a warm greenhouse, and in seven weeks' time the perfect insects appeared. They were like small dragonflies, with slender bodies, four black-spotted gauzy wings, two large black eyes and short antennae.

I had read about their being nocturnal insects, feeding on flies, so they had that diet provided for them in the glass globe in which they were kept, but I could never feel sure that they ate the flies, and fearing they would be starved I tried giving them a little sweet food, a drop of raspberry syrup at the end of a twig; it seemed to be the right thing, for they greedily sucked it in, but in spite of all my care they only lived four weeks; which, however, is probably the term of their existence.

Whilst I was writing this paper a singular incident occurred. I heard a strange, wild note, and something brilliant dashed past me to the end of the room, and there, on a white marble bust sat a lovely kingfisher a bird I had hardly ever seen, even at a distance, and here he had come to pay me a visit in my drawing-room. Would that I could have told him how welcome he was! but, alas! he darted about the room in wild alarm, flew against the looking-glasses, and though I tried to guard him from a plate-glass window, that has often proved fatal to birds, I was too late; he came with a crash against it and fell down quite dead, his neck being broken by the force of the blow.

I had heard that a kingfisher had been seen at my lake, and hoped that the bird might build and become established there; it was, therefore, a keen regret to me that this bright visitant had met with such an untimely fate.

ROBINS I HAVE KNOWN.

IF I once begin to speak about these winning, confiding little birds, I shall hardly know when to stop. There can scarcely be a more delightful pet than a wild robin which has learnt to love you, and will come indoors and be your quiet companion for hours together. One can feel happy in the thought that he has his liberty and his natural food out of doors, and that he gives you his companionship freely because he likes to be with you, and shows that he does, by singing his sweet songs perched on the looking-glass or some vase of flowers.

Autumn is the best time to begin taming such a little friend. When one of those brown-coated young birds in his first year's plumage (before the red feathers show) takes to haunting the windowledge, or looks up inquiringly from the gravel path outside, then is the time to throw out a mealworm, four or five times a day, when the bird appears. He will soon associate you with his pleasant diet, and come nearer, and grow daily less fearful, until, by putting mealworms on a mat just inside the room, he will come in and take them, and at last learn to be quite content to remain. The first few times the window should be left open to let him retreat, for unless he feels he can come and go at will he will probably make a dash at a closed window, not seeing the glass, and be fatally injured, or else too frightened to return.

Like all other taming, it must be carried on with patience.

One summer, many years ago, we occupied an old-fashioned house in the country, where, in perfect quietude, one could make acquaintance with birds and study their habits and manners without interruption. From the veranda of a large, low-ceilinged sitting-room one looked out upon a garden of the olden type, full of moss-grown apple-trees, golden daffodils, lupines and sweet herbs, that pleasant mixture of the kitchen and flower garden which always seems so enjoyable. It was an ideal home for birds, no cat was ever visible, and from the numbers of the feathered folk one could believe that countless generations had been reared in these apple-trees and lived out their little lives in perfect happiness. I soon found a friend amongst the robins; one in particular began to pay me frequent visits as I sat at work indoors. At first he ventured in rather timidly, took a furtive glance and then flew away, but finding that crumbs were scattered for him, and while he picked them up a kindly voice encouraged his advances, he soon became at ease, made his way into the room and seemed to examine by turns, with birdish curiosity, all the pieces of furniture and the various ornaments on the mantelpiece and tables. Much to my pleasure he began to sing to me, and very pretty he looked, sitting amongst the flowers in a tall vase, warbling his charming little ditty, keeping his large black eyes fixed upon me as if to see if I seemed impressed by his vocal efforts.

Once he stopped in the middle of his song, looked keenly at a corner of the ceiling, and after a swift flight there, he returned with a spider in his beak; one can well believe what good helpers the insect-eating birds must be to the gardener, by destroying countless hosts of minute caterpillars and grubs that would otherwise prey upon the garden produce. Bobbie continued his visits to me throughout the summer, remaining happy and content for hours at a time, pluming himself, singing, and at times investigating the contents of a little cupboard, where he sometimes discovered a cake which was much to his taste, on which he feasted without any leave asked, though truly it would have been readily given to such a pleasant little visitor. He soon showed such entire confidence in me that he would perch on the book I was reading, and alight on my lap for crumbs even when many people were in the room.

When we had to leave this country home I wished that dear Bobbie could have been packed up to go elsewhere with our other possessions, but since this could not be, let us hope he still inhabits the old garden and cheers other home-dwellers with his confiding manners and morning and evening songs of praise.

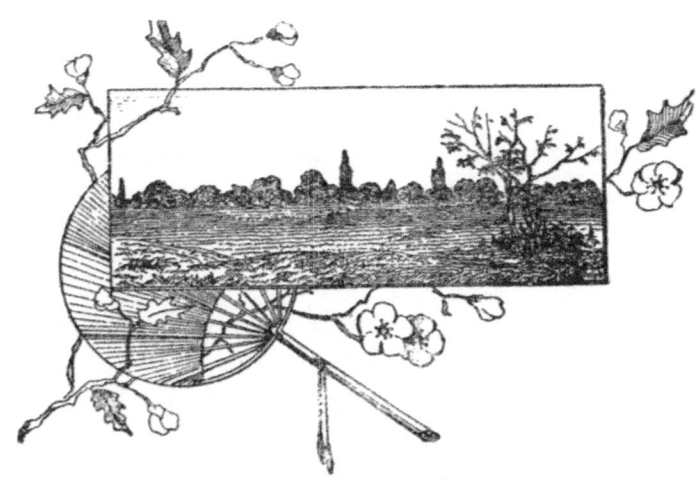

ROBERT THE SECOND.

AFTER slight intimacies with various robins who were visitors to the conservatory and found their way in and out at the open windows, I was led to special friendship with a brown-coated young bird I used often to see close to the open French window where I was sitting. He was coaxed into the room by mealworms being thrown to him until he made himself quite at home indoors. By the time he had attained his red breast the weather had become too cold for open windows, but Bobbie would sit on the ledge and wait till I let him in, and then he would be my happy little companion for the whole morning, flitting all about the room, along the corridor, into the hall in fact, he was to be found all over the house; but when hungry he returned to me as his best friend, because I was the provider of his delightsome mealworms. It was always amusing to visitors to see me feed my small fowl! He would be on the alert to see where his prey was to be found, and he would hunt for it perseveringly if it happened to fall out of sight. He was often to be seen perched on the Californian mouse's cage, and I wondered what could be the attraction; at last I discovered that he coveted mousie's brown biscuits, and after that he was allowed one for his own use, kept in a special corner, where a cup of water was also provided for his small requirements.

However tame wild birds may seem there will be times when all at once a sort of intense longing to get out seems to possess them. When this was the case Bobbie would fly backwards and forwards uttering his plaintive cry (one of the six kinds of notes by which robins express their feelings), and his distress was so evident that the window was always opened at once to let him go out.

I am sorry to have to confess that robins are most vindictive towards each other! Bobbie maintained a very angry warfare with a hated rival out-of-doors, in fact his chief occupation in life seemed to be watching for his enemy. He might often be seen sitting under a small palm in a pot on the window-ledge, and whilst looking the picture of gentle innocence he was, I fear, cherishing envy, hatred, and malice in his naughty little heart, for, all at once, there would be a grand fluttering and pecking at the window whilst the two little furies, one inside and the other out, expended their strength in harmless warfare which only ceased when they were too exhausted to do more, and then followed on both sides a triumphant song of defiance or victory.

I must now weave into this biography the life-history of a poor robin which, I suppose, must have been caught in a trap, for it had lost the lower mandible of its beak, and had only a little knob remaining of the upper mandible. It haunted the windows, and looked so hungry and miserable from its inability to pick up its food, that I thought it kindest to coax it into a cage where it could be fed with suitable food. By placing mealworms in a cage I at last induced it to hop in, and for five months it had a very happy life indoors, feeding on soaked brown bread and all the insect-diet I could secure for it When the cage was cleaned each morning Bobbie was let out, and would take a bath in a glass dish, and then fly to the top of the looking-glass, where he would often remain all day unless we were quick enough to secure his cage-door when he went in to feed. By the middle of May I thought caterpillars would be plentiful enough for him to find his own living, so one day he was released, but unhappily Robert the Second was close by, and the moment he saw the invalid in his cage on the lawn with the door open, he rushed in and savagely fought the poor defenceless bird. Before we could interfere he drove our pet out of his cage, and terrible was the battle that went on; the beakless bird was driven far away, and I was quite unhappy about his fate, for he was now beyond my loving care, and I never expected to see him again. Two months passed by, and I only once caught a glimpse of the invalid, but at last he came just as before to the window, looking thin and ill, with ruffled feathers, and evidently again at starvation point. Once more he entered his cage and began his old life, only now he was hung under the veranda so as to enjoy fresh air and the songs of his companions. For two months I endeavoured to keep the dear little creature happy; we were all so fond of him, and it seems very touching to think that in his times of extremity he should have come willingly into captivity and felt sure that a kind welcome would be accorded him. But no amount of care could bring him through the moulting season, the lack of a beak to plume his feathers and his great difficulty in picking up even the mealworms made him weak and sickly. He got out of his cage one day into the garden, and a few days after we found his poor little body lying dead close to the window where he had always found the help he needed, and yet we could not but be glad that his sorrowful little life was ended.

When robins have been thus tamed for years the families they rear are like pet birds; they are fed by their parents close to the windows, and then come indoors, as if they knew they would be welcome everywhere.

There is one feature in the robin's character that, as far as I know, is shared by no other bird; I mean his adopting a certain spot as his district and always keeping to it, just as the stickle-backs portion out a pond and jealously defend the territory they have chosen. Here, there is a special robin to be found at each of the lodges; one haunts the Mission Hall and will often sing vigorously from the reading-stand while classes are going on. A very tame one lives in the coachman's house, running about the floor like a little brown mouse, and sitting inside the fender on cold days to warm himself. He must have met with trouble in his early youth, for when first seen he was very lame, and had lost the sight of one eye. Through kind care he has become well and strong, but he is much at the mercy of his enemies, who often attack, him on his blind side. The conservatory, dining-room, and drawing-rooms have each their little redbreast visitor; the latter is so tame he will take meal-worms from my hand, and sits on my inkstand singing a sweet, low song whilst I write. As long as each bird keeps to his domain there is peace, but woe to any intruder! The conflicts are desperate, and I have often to mediate, and separate two little furies rolling over and over on the ground. I suppose it is in this way that the idea has arisen about the young robins killing the old ones; I cannot ascertain that it has any foundation in fact, every robin fights his neighbour all the year through, except when paired and busy with domestic duties. As dead redbreasts are not found specially in autumn, I do not think there can be any truth in the superstition.

FEEDING BIRDS IN SUMMER AND WINTER

ON wintry mornings, when leaf and twig are decked with hoar-frost and the ground is hard and dry, affording no food for the birds, it is a piteous sight to see them cowering under the evergreens with ruffled feathers, evidently starving and miserable, quietly waiting for the death that must overtake many of them unless we come to their rescue.

It is one of my delights to feed the small "feathered fowls" through all the winter months, and I only wish all my readers could enjoy with me the lovely scenes of happy bird life to be witnessed through the French window opposite my writing-table. These gatherings of birds are the result of many years of persistent kindness and thought for the welfare of my bird pets. Their tameness cannot be attained all at once; it takes time to establish confidence; it needs thought about the kinds of food required by various species of birds, regularity in feeding, and quiet gentleness of manner to avoid frightening any new and timid visitors. Doubtless there are very many lovers of birds who share this pleasure with me, but for those who may not happen to know how to attract the feathered tribes I will go a little into detail.

This being a large garden near game preserves, and surrounded by a wide, furze-covered common, I have been able to attract and tame the ordinary wild pheasants by putting out Indian corn, buckwheat, and raisins, till now they come to the doorstep and look up with their brilliant, red-ringed eyes, and feed calmly whilst I watch them. It is a really beautiful sight to see three or four cock birds, with their golden-bronze plumage glistening like polished metal as the morning sun rests upon them, and as many of their more sober-coloured mates feasting on the dainties they find prepared for them; as a rule, they are very amicable and feed together like barndoor fowls. When satisfied, the brown hens run swiftly away to cover, while the cocks, with greater confidence, walk quietly away in stately fashion, or remain under the trees.

Wood-pigeons are usually very shy and wary birds, yet these also come, six and eight at a time, and feed at my window, Indian corn and peas being their specialities. I have large quantities of beech-nuts and acorns collected every autumn, and thus I can scatter this food also for pigeons and squirrels ail through the winter. Jays, jackdaws, rooks, and magpies also approve of acorns and beech-nuts, so it is doing a real kindness to tribes of birds to reserve this food for them until their other stores are exhausted, and we can thus bring them within our view and study their interesting ways, their modes of feeding, and, I fear I must add, their squabbles also, for hungry birds are very pugnacious.

Blackbirds and thrushes are very fond of Sultana raisins; they also like split groats and brown bread crumbs, as also do starlings and, I believe, most of the smaller birds. Fat in any shape or form will attract the various species of titmice to the window. I always keep a small Normandy basket full of suet and ham-fat hanging on a nail at the window. It is a great rendezvous for these charming little pets, and it is also supplied with Barcelona nuts for nuthatches, who fully appreciate them and carry them off to the nearest tree with rugged bark into which they fix the nuts, and then hammer at the shell till they can extract the contents.

In very hard frosts I used always to put out a pan of water, as I feared the birds suffered from thirst and needed this help. One day, however, I was comforted to see some starlings, after a good meal of groats, run off to the grass plot and eagerly peck at the hoar-frost, which, while it exists, thus supplies the lack of water.

Bewick says linnets are so named from their fondness for linseed, and I think most of the finches like it. The greenfinch is soon attracted by hemp seed, and all the smaller birds by canary seed. I hope this paper may induce many kind hands to minister to the needs of our feathered friends during the winter months. It is sad to think of their dying for lack of the food we can so easily afford them, and they will be sure to repay us by their sweet songs and confiding tameness when summer days return. One is apt to think that winter is the only time when birds need our help and bounty, but there is almost as much real distress after a long drought in summer, especially amongst the insect-eating birds.

I was led to think of this by the pathetic way in which a hen blackbird came to the French window of my room early in June last and stood patiently waiting and clicking time after time in trouble of *some* kind I knew, and, supposing it might be food, I threw out a plentiful supply of soaked brown bread. At once the poor bird went to it, devouring ravenously for her own needs, and then, filling her beak as full as it would hold, she flew off with a supply for her young brood. Then came thrushes, robins, sparrows, a whole bevy of feathered folk all doing the same thing–carrying the provisions in every direction for unseen families at starvation point, and I began to realize that the month of continued sunshine in which we had rejoiced had brought great distress upon the birds by drying up the lawns so that no worms could be found, and, as it was early in the year, but few insects were to be had, so that just when each pair of birds had a clamorous brood to provide for the food supply had fallen short Now I understood the pathos of the hen blackbird's appeal; her dark eyes and note of distress were trying to say to me, "I know you care for us; you seemed so kind last winter; when we were without food you fed us and saved our lives; but now 1 am in far deeper distress my children are crying for food, the grass is dried up, and the ground so hard that I cannot find a single worm, I am thin and worn with hunger myself; do help me and my little ones, and we will sing you sweet songs in return to cheer you when wintry days come back again. Does she understand? I've said all this several times before, but I thought I would make one last appeal before my children die. Yes; she has left the room! I will wait Ah! here it is, just the soft food that will suit my little ones: how they *will* rejoice and all want to be fed at once. I hope my friend can understand that I am thanking her with all my heart." Love has a universal language and can interpret through varied signs, and thus I quite believe the mother bird's heart wished to express itself.

Ever since that day I have been careful in nesting time to supply suitable and varied food for the families of young birds in times of drought, for it seems mournful to think of their dying from want, in the season of flowers and green leaves, when nature is to us so attractive, and rendered all the more so by their sweet songs.

RAB, MINOR.

THIS familiar name recalls the delightful story of "Rab and his Friends" in "Horæ Subsicivæ," with its naive description of a very original "tyke" of a doggie—a biography which had so lived in my recollection that when a queer little fluffy dumpling of a puppy was given me I could not help giving it the old familiar name, little knowing how aptly true the name would prove to be in after years.

Is there anything more comical than a young Scotch terrier puppy, with its preternatural gravity, its queer, ungainly attempts at play, its tumbles, and blue-eyed simplicity, and, best of all, its sage look, with head on one side, trying to consider the merits of some doggie idea which is puzzling his infant brain? Rab went through all the stages of puppyhood, showing the usual amount of mischief and fun; he might be met carrying about some unfortunate slipper frayed to pieces by his busy teeth, or burying a favourite bone under a wool mat in the drawing-room, or, worse still, it is recorded in domestic chronicles that he buried a hymn-book in the garden, whereupon the cook remarked that she believed he had more religion in him than half the Christians; but that reasoning was not apparent to any one but herself.

Rab's most notable adventures took place after he had emerged from puppyhood. He had a most indomitable spirit of disobedience; he would hunt rabbits or anything else he could find in the woods, and one day he reached home with a snare tightly drawn round his neck, and panting distressingly for breath; the wire was cut only just in time to save his life.

Another time he was poisoned by something he had eaten, and had a long suffering illness.

His fights with other dogs were fierce and frequent, and whilst engaged in a scrimmage with a hated rival, Rab was run over by a passing cart, and limped home in a very dejected state; no bones were broken, but he was an invalid for some months in consequence.

At last it was thought needful to tie him up, and he had his appointed house and a long chain, and with frequent exercise he became quite content. One morning our brave little friend was found nearly dead, with two terrible wounds in his neck, which must have been made by a sharp knife, driven twice through his throat, but, strangely enough, had each time just missed severing the wind-pipe. He had nearly died from loss of blood, and was scarcely able to breathe; still, our kind servants did not give him up; warm milk and beef tea were given him constantly through the day; and by night he had revived a little, and was evidently going to live. We could never trace the origin of this outrage, and could only suppose that burglars had purposed breaking into our house, and, enraged at Rab's barking, had at last got hold of, and, as they thought, killed him, and flung the body into an adjoining field. Poor little doggie! he suffered grievously for his brave defence, and for months the wounds were a great distress to him and to us; but all that loving care could do was done, and once more his wonderful constitution enabled him to regain health and strength. We kept at that time several very large mastiffs, and the next adventure occurred early one morning, when we were aroused by a terrific noise in the stable-yard, and the message brought to us was to the effect that Rab was quite dead. He had been worried by one of the mastiffs which had got loose in the night I rose quickly and went to see the poor little victim's body, and looking at it, I saw a little quiver in the eyelid that led to a gleam of hope. I had him carried indoors, and again teaspoons of milk, &c., were given, and actually he began to revive, and a feeble wag of his tail seemed to say, "I'm very bad, but not dead yet." The sad part was that the shaking and worrying he had received had reopened the previous wounds, and though after a time he was able to get about, he was quite a wreck; one ear was gone, and the other, strange to say, was but a fragment, like his namesake in "Rab and his Friends." Still, he lived to be nearly fifteen, and then rheumatism and loss of teeth made his life a distress to him, and he was peacefully dismissed to the rest he had bravely earned by his life of courageous devotion to what he thought the path of duty.

A VISIT TO JAMRACH.

THERE is an old and true saying–"Everything comes to him who waits." I thought of this saying while on my way to visit the well-known place near the London Docks where Mr. Jamrach is supposed to keep almost every rare animal, bird, and reptile, ready to supply the wants of all customers at a moment's notice. For many long years I had wished to pay him a visit, but ill-health and other causes had proved a hindrance and I could hardly believe my wish was going to be realized when I found myself on the way to his menagerie. After driving through a labyrinth of narrow, dirty streets, we were at last obliged to get out and walk till we came to the shop, and then we did indeed find ourselves in the midst of "animated nature." We had landed amongst the cockatoos, macaws, and parrots, and they greeted our arrival with such a chorus of shrieks, screams, and hideous cries that my first desire was to rush away anywhere out of the reach of such ear-piercing sounds. One had to bear it, however, if the curious creatures in the various cages were to be examined, and after a time the uproar grew less, and I could hear a word or two from Mr. Jamrach, who called my attention to some armadillos, huge armour-plated animals, very curious, but somehow not attractive as pets; one could not fondle a thing composed of metal plates, shaped like a pig, with a tendency to roll itself up into a ball on the slightest provocation, and even Mr. Jamrach's argument that if I got tired of it as a pet I could have it cooked, as they were excellent eating, failed to lead me to a purchase. There was a fine, healthy toucan, with his marvellous bill, looking sadly out of place in a small cage in such a dingy place. Did he ever think of his tropical forest home, I wondered, and wish himself in happier surroundings? A long wooden box with wire front contained rows and rows of Grass Parrakeets: many hundreds must have been on those perches, one behind the other, poor little patient birdies, sitting in solemn silence, never moving an inch, for they were wedged in as closely as they could sit and how they could eat and live seemed a mystery. As I was in quest of some small rodents I was asked to follow Mr. Jamrach to another place where the animals were kept. We came to a back yard with dens and cages containing all kinds of tenants, from fierce hyenas and wolves to tame deer, monkeys, cats, and dogs. A chorus of yelps and barks and growls sounded a little uninviting, and a caution from Jamrach, to mind the camel did not seize my young friend's hat, made us aware of a stately form gazing down upon us from a recess we had not before noticed. Every nook and corner seemed occupied, and in order to see a kangaroo rat I was invited up a rickety ladder into a loft where a Japanese cat, a large monkey, and sundry other creatures lived. I did not take to the kangaroo rat, he was too large and formidable to be pleasant, and was by no means tame, but to be pulled out of the cage by his long tail was, I confess, enough to scare the mildest quadruped. At length I was shown some Peruvian guinea-pigs. Wonderful little creatures! With hair three or four inches long, white, yellow and black, set on anyhow, sticking out in odd tufts, one side of their heads white and the other black, their eyes just like boot buttons, they were captivating; and a pair had to be chosen forthwith, and packed in a basket with a tortoise and a huge Egyptian lizard, and with these spoils I was not sorry to leave this place of varied noises and smells. The lizard was about fourteen inches long, a really grand creature. He came from the ruins of ancient Egypt, and looked in his calm stateliness as though he might have gazed upon the Pharaohs themselves. When placed in the sun for a time he would sometimes deign to move a few inches, his massive, grey, scaly body looking very like a young crocodile. I was greatly teased about my fondness for "Rameses," as I called this new and majestic pet; there was a great fascination about him, and as I really wished to know more of his ways and habits, I carried the basket in which he lived everywhere with me indoors and out, and studied all possible ways of feeding him; but alas! nothing would induce him to eat. After gazing for five minutes at the most tempting mealworm, he would at last raise up his mighty head and appeal to be revolving great ideas to which mealworms and all sublunary things must give place. Jamrach told me that the lizard would drink milk, so a saucerful was placed before him, and once he did drink a few drops, but generally he walked into and over the saucer as if it did not exist.

I believe the poor creature had been without food so long that it had lost the power of taking nourishment, and to my great regret I found it grew weaker and thinner, and at last it died, and all I could do was to send the remains to a naturalist to be preserved somewhat after the fashion of its great namesake.

The odd little guinea-pigs were named Fluff and Jamrach, and were a source of much amusement. As they could not agree, and as the fights grew serious, Jamrach was banished to the stable and Fluff occupied a cage in the dining-room. When let out it was curious to see how he would always keep close to the sides of the room never would he venture into the middle, the protection of the skirting board seemed indispensable, and when let out under the tulip-tree he ran round the trunk in the same way, only occasionally making an excursion to the edge of the branches which rested on the ground, the space beyond was a *terra incognita* which could not be explored by the timid little beastie.

There the two little guinea-pigs enjoyed a happy life on fine days and grew to be friends at last, grunting little confidences one to the other and going to sleep side by side. They had to be watched and their liberty a good deal curtailed when we found a weasel began to appear upon the scene, and as it is proverbially difficult to catch a weasel either awake or asleep, he has not at present been captured. I much fear if he ever attacked the little Peruvians they would stand a poor chance of their lives, for they have no idea of self-defence and would fall an easy prey to such a fierce, relentless persecutor. Perhaps the gardener may devise some way of trapping the wary little creature, so that my little friends may dwell in peace under the shady tree.

As the winter came on the cold prevented Fluff going out-of-doors, and he led a most inactive life. I don't think he ever had more than two ideas in his little brain he just lived to eat and sleep, and was about as interesting as a stuffed animal would have been. He is the only instance of any animal I have ever known who seemed to be literally without a single habit, apparently without affection, without a temper good or bad, with no wishes or desires except to be let alone to doze away his aimless life.

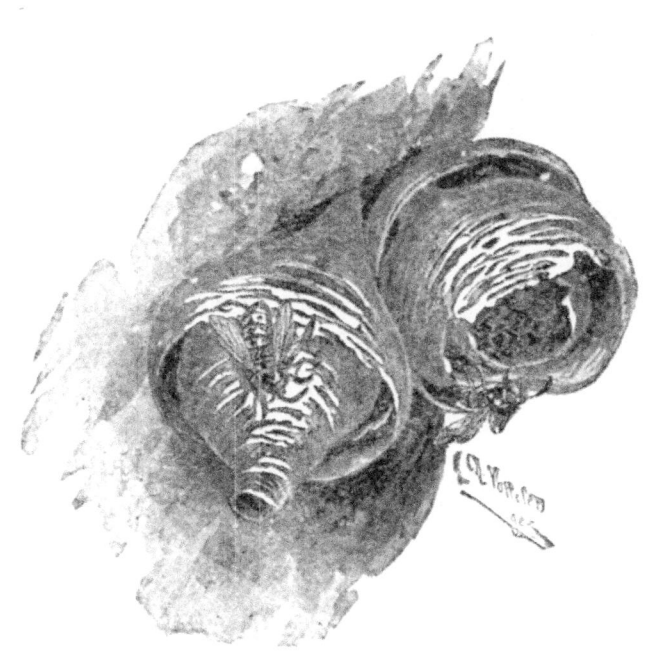

HOW TO OBSERVE NATURE

THERE is all the difference between taking a walk simply for exercise, for some special errand, or to enjoy conversation with one's friends, and the sort of quiet observant stroll I am going to ask my kind readers to take with me to-day.

This beautiful world is full of wonders of every kind, full of evidences of the Great Creator's wisdom and skill in adapting each created thing to its special purpose. The whole realm of nature is meant, I believe, to speak to us, to teach us lessons in parables to lead our hearts upward to God who made us and fitted us also for our special place in creation.

In the nineteenth Psalm David speaks of the two great books God has given us for our instruction. In the first six verses he speaks of the teachings of the book of nature and the rest of the Psalm deals with the written Word of God.

We acknowledge and read the Scriptures as the book which reveals the will of God and His wondrous works for the welfare of mankind, but how many fail to give any time or thought to reading the book of nature! Thousands may travel and admire beautiful scenery, and derive a certain amount of pleasure from nature, just glancing at each object, but really observing nothing, and thus failing to learn any of the lessons this world's beauty is intended to teach, they might almost as well have stayed at home save for the benefit of fresh air and change of scene. The habit of minute and careful observation is seldom taught in childhood, and is not very likely to be gained in later life when the mind is filled with other things. Yet if natural objects are presented attractively to the young, how quickly they are interested! Question after question is asked, and unconsciously a vast amount of information may be conveyed to an intelligent child's mind by a simple, happy little chat about some bird or insect. This is admirably shown in a chapter on Education in the Life of Mrs. Sewell. I would strongly urge every mother to read and follow the advice there given.

We will now start for our garden walk. We have not taken many steps before we are led to pause and inquire why there should be little patches of grey-looking mud in the small angles of the brickwork of the house. Opening one of the patches with a penknife we find a hollow cell, and in it some green caterpillars just alive but not able to crawl. Now I see that the cell is the work of one of the solitary mason wasps; she brings the material, forms the cell, and when nearly finished lays her egg at the bottom and provides these half-killed caterpillars as food for the young grub when it is hatched, and by the time they are eaten the grub becomes a pupa and then hatches into a young wasp to begin life on its own account. One day I saw a bee go into a hole in the brickwork of the house, and getting my net I waited to capture it; after about five minutes the bee came out and flew into the net. It proved to be a solitary mason bee, and was doubtless forming a place to lay its egg, only, unlike the wasp, she would give the young grub pollen from the stamens of flowers to feed upon instead of green caterpillars. I remember seeing a mass of clay which had been formed into a wasp's nest by one of the solitary species, under the flap of a pembroke table in an unused room. A maid in dusting lifted up the flap, and down fell a quantity of fine, dry mud with young grubs in it which would soon have hatched into wasps, and revealed their rather strange nesting-place. I have in my collection a very interesting hornet's nest, which was being constructed in the hollow of an old tree. I happened to notice a hornet fly into the opening, and, looking in, there was a small beginning of a nest. It hung from a kind of stalk and consisted of only eight cells, each having an egg at the bottom. I captured the two hornets, and though I watched for a long time no others ever came, so I imagine they were the founders of what would have been a colony in due time.

But we have been kept a long time engaged with these mason wasps. Let us start for our walk. As we take our way through the garden we cannot help noticing the happy songs of the different birds, all in full activity preparing their nests, carolling to their mates or seeking food for the little ones. There is a loud tapping noise as we pass an old fir-tree, but no bird is to be seen, so we go round to the other side and trace the noise to a small hole near which a quantity of congealed turpentine shows that the bark has been pierced by a woodpecker and the sap is oozing out. I rap outside the hole and in a minute the grey head of a nuthatch appears. He is evidently chiselling out a "highly desirable residence" for his summer quarters in this cosy nook, and the hole being so small he will not need to get clay to reduce the size of the opening and plaster in his mate, which is said to be the curious habit of this bird. Do you see that hole about forty feet up the stem of the beech opposite? A nuthatch built there six years ago; I often watched him going in and out, and heard his peculiar cry as he brought food for his mate and her young ones. Next year that lodging was taken by a starling, who reared a brood there. The year after the nuthatch had it, and then a jackdaw built there; and each year I always feel interested to see who the lodgers are going to be.

When I was rearing the wild ducks already described, a weasel used often to be prowling near the coop, and when frightened retreated in this direction. It happened one day I was walking softly on the grass and saw the weasel playing and frisking at the root of that young tree; one seldom has such an opportunity of seeing it, for it is very shy and has wonderfully quick hearing. It was seeking about in the grass, leaping here and there, snuffing the wind, with its snake-like, wicked-looking head raised to see over the grass stems, and thus at last it caught sight of me, and in a second it darted into the hole you see there, and I thus learnt where he lived, but I have not been able to trace his history any further at present.

Did you see that snake? We have many of them on the common, and they often cross my path in the garden. Happily there are not many of the venomous kind: they are smaller than this one, and have a V-shaped mark on the head. One day in August I was sitting by the open French window in the drawing-room when one of these harmless snakes came close to me, looked up at me, putting its quivering little tongue in and out I suppose it decided that I could be trusted, for it glided in and coiled itself round upon my dress skirt and seemed to go to sleep. I let it stay a good while, but fearing some one might be frightened at seeing it there, I reached my parasol and with the hooked handle softly took up the snake and laid it on the grass-plat outside thinking it would go away but no, it only turned round and came back and coiled itself up in the same place. I found it did not mind being touched, so I stroked it and made it creep all its length through my hand not a very pleasant sensation, but a curious experience rarely to be met with. When the cold, clammy creature had passed out of my hand it threw out a most disgusting odour, of which I had often read. I imagine it was offended at my touching it and did this in self defence. I had at last to carry it a long distance to ensure it should not return to the room again.

Some years ago I was witness to the mode in which a snake pursues its victim. A large frog leaped upon the gravel walk before the windows, crying piteously like a child and taking rapid leaps; a moment after a large snake appeared swiftly pursuing the frog. At last it reached it, and gave it a bite which broke its back, and then, being alarmed, it darted away amongst some rock-work, leaving the frog in a dying state.

This bank we are passing is a favourite winter retreat for female humble bees. Early in the autumn they begin to scoop out a little tunnel in this grassy slope, and when it is deep enough to protect them from the frost they retire into it, and pushing up the earth behind them close up the entrance of the hole, and there lie dormant until the warmth of spring tempts them to come out. Then they may be found in great numbers on the early sallow, and other tree-blossoms, recruiting their strength, while they seek a place in some hedge-bank wherein to found a new colony.

The Carder bee forms its nest on the ground and makes a roof of interwoven moss, from which it takes its name. I once gathered the moss from such a nest by chance and saw the little mass of cells with honey in them. I went away, meaning to examine it more closely on my return, but a crow in the apple-tree overhead chanced to spy the nest and made off with it in his beak before I could rescue the honey store of the poor little bees I had so unwittingly injured.

That old tree-stump is being gradually carried away by wasps. The wood is just sufficiently decayed to afford the material of which they make their nests. You see there are several wasps busily rasping pieces of the rotten wood into convenient-sized morsels, which they can carry to the nest, there to be masticated into the papery layers of which the outer walls of the nest are formed. This walk used to have a row of grand old silver firs of great height, but each winter some of them have been blown down till only a few are left.

Some years since I noticed at the root of one of them a pile of fine sawdust more than a foot high, and found that some wood wasps were busily engaged in excavating the interior of the tree and forming tunnels in which to lay their eggs. I watched them for half an hour and found that every half-minute a wasp went in at the aperture carrying a blue-bottle or some kind of fly in its mandibles. Next day I took a friend to see the wasps, and while watching them the wind caused the immense tree-stem to sway to and fro from its base as if in the act of falling, and on examination we found it was only held in its place by a small portion of root, and though the branches were green, it must have been hollow and dead inside, which appears to be the way in which silver firs decay, and the wasps had found it out and made a delightful home in the rotten wood. With some difficulty the great tree was safely taken down, and then it was a most curious sight to see the endless chambers and galleries made in the stem, all tenanted by young wasp-grubs and half-dead flies; and all the summer they were being hatched in countless numbers. The view over our common is lovely from this point; it is golden with rich yellow gorse, giving cover to innumerable rabbits, which find their way into our garden in spite of wire fences and all that the gardener can do to keep them out. One clever little mother rabbit made her burrow deep down in a heap of sawdust close to the stable. My coachman put his arm down to the bottom of the hole and brought out a little grey furred creature, kicking and screaming with wonderful vigour in spite of its tender years. The nest was allowed to remain, and in a few days the mother removed her brood to a hole at the root of a bushy stone-pine, where the little ones frisked in and out and looked so pretty that I was won over to allow them to stay, and, by netting round the tree, we formed a miniature warren for the young family; but I fear that in course of time we may bitterly repent this step, and the numbers may increase to such an extent that pinks and lobelia may become things of the past and the rabbit warren may have to be abolished.

A fox is sometimes seen and hunted in these parts. One surprised me by leaping upon the window-sill and looking into the drawing-room. At first I could not think what it was. It had been dug out of its hole; its fur was muddy and torn, its eyes piteous in their expression, and when it ran slowly on I saw it was very lame. I ran to the window to let it in, but though it leaped up to each window in succession, they all happened to be shut, and I was quite grieved to think the poor, weary creature could find no shelter. I am no admirer of field-sports. I think they give rise to the utmost cruelty to the creatures hunted and shot, to the horses and dogs employed; and to witness torture inflicted on unoffending animals cannot but have a debasing effect on the human mind. When once any one has seen the anguish of a deer, a fox, or hare, at the end of the race, there can be no question about the cruelty of the proceeding, and to one who loves every created thing as I do, it gives the keenest pain to know how much suffering of this kind goes on during the hunting season.[1]

There goes a cuckoo, with quite a flight of small birds pursuing him wherever he goes.

Small birds seem to have an intense hatred of jays and cuckoos, and will often fly at them in the nesting season, giving them no peace till they drive them out of the garden, knowing full well that their own broods are often devoured by the jay, and that the cuckoo has designs upon the nests.

Although we are some distance from home, I can show you one of my own bees on this furze blossom. I have a hive of Swiss, or Ligurian bees, which are said to be in some respects superior to the English species. The honey is of excellent flavour, and the first year

---

[1] I cannot resist quoting and strongly endorsing the following lament by Mr. H. Stacy Marks, R.A., as to the way in which birds are too frequently treated by the public at large: "Many people regarding birds in but three aspects as things to be either eaten, shot, or worn.... No natural history of a bird is complete without recording where the last specimen was shot; and should a rare bird visit our shores, the hospitality which we accord to the foreign refugee is denied, and it is bound to be the victim of powder and shot. The fashion of wearing birds or their plumage as part of ladies' attire, threatens to exterminate many beautiful species, such as the humming-birds of South America, the glossy starlings of Africa, and the glorious Impeyan pheasant of the Himalayas, with many other species."

I had far more honey from the Ligurian hive. I do not think any other hives of Ligurians are kept within five miles, and, as you see, they have a band of bright yellow on the abdomen. I can always tell my own bees when I meet with them in my walks on the common or in the lanes. I had a rather trying adventure with these bees last May. One Sunday evening we were just starting for church, about half-past six, when my little niece ran in exclaiming that there was a great bunch of bees hanging on a branch near the hives. I knew what had happened my very irreverent bees had swarmed on this quiet Sunday evening, and they must be hived if possible.

My bonnet was soon off and the bee-dress put on, and in five minutes the bees were secured and settled into a hive. We went to church and were not even late, but during the first prayer I heard ominous sounds of a furious bee under my dress; it was, fortunately, a partly transparent material, and glancing furtively about I saw my little friend under the skirt going up and down with an angry biz-z-z. Only the pocket-hole could release him, so I held that safely in my hand all through the service, lest the congregation might suffer the wrath of a furious bee, which in truth is no light matter, for in blind fury it will rush at the first person it meets and leave its sting in the face or hand. Happily I succeeded in bringing the bee home again, and resolved to avoid hiving swarms before church-time in future.

You see under the drooping boughs of the fir-tree yonder an old stone basin, well known to all the birds in the neighbourhood, for there they always find a supply of fresh water and food of various kinds to suit all tastes. As it is opposite the dining-room window, it is very interesting to see a tame jay and sundry squirrels enjoying the acorns which were collected for them last autumn and stored up so as to keep the basin well supplied all through the winter and spring, until other food should be plentiful. Finches, robins, and sparrows find wheat and crumbs to their taste, and take their daily bath not without some squabbling as to who shall have it first a difficulty which is sometimes settled by a portly blackbird appearing on the scene and scattering the smaller folk, whilst he takes his early tubbing and sends up showers of spray in the process. Very pretty are the scenes on that same stone basin when in early summer a mother bird brings her little tribe of downy, chirping babes, and feeds each little gaping mouth with some suitable morsels from the store she finds there.

A sheaf of corn in winter is also a great boon to the starved-out birdies, when snow has long deprived them of their natural food, and the water supply has to be often renewed on freezing days, for many a bird dies in winter from lack of water, all its usual supplies being frozen. The tameness of birds in severe weather is a touching sign of their distress, and a mute appeal to us to help them.

> "The fowls of heaven
> Tam'd by the cruel season, crowd around
> The winnowing store, and claim the little boon
> Which Providence assigns them."

It is pleasant to think that they seldom appeal in vain. "Crumbs for the birds" are scattered by kindly little hands everywhere in winter, and in many a house a pet sonsie little robin is a cherished visitor, always welcome to his small share of the good things of this life.

Our ramble might be indefinitely prolonged and still be full of interest and instruction, but in these simple remarks enough has been shown, I trust, to lead many to think and observe closely every, even the minutest, thing that catches their attention whilst out for a ramble in lanes and fields, even a microscopic moss upon an old wall has been suggestive of many lovely thoughts, with which I will conclude our ramble and this chapter.

"It was not all a tale of eld,
  That fairies, who their revels held
  By moonlight, in the greenwood shade
  Their beakers of the moss-cups made.
  The wondrous light which science burns
  Reveals those lovely jewelled urns!
  Fair lace-work spreads from roughest stems
  And shows each tuft a mine of gems.
    Voices from the silent sod,
    Speaking of the Perfect God,

  Fringeless, or fringed, and fringed again,
  No single leaflet formed in vain;
  What wealth of heavenly wisdom lies
  Within one moss-cup's mysteries!
  And few may know what silvery net,
  Down in its mimic depths is set
  To catch the rarest dews that fall
  Upon the dry and barren wall.
    Voices from the silent sod,
    Speaking of the Perfect God."

L.N.R.

End

Made in the USA
Las Vegas, NV
28 August 2024

94535238R10080